7 Keys to Answered Prayer

Robert R. Thibodeau

7 Keys to Answered Prayer

Unless otherwise stated, all Scripture quotations are taken from the King James Version of the Bible.

Freedom Through Faith Ministries
PO Box 4936
Middle River, MD 21220
www.ftfm.org

Copyright © 2011 by Robert Thibodeau and
Freedom Through Faith Ministries
All Rights Reserved

All rights reserved. Printed in the United States of America. No part of this book may be reproduced in any manner whatsoever without written permission except in case of brief quotations embodied in critical articles and reviews. For permissions, please contact Freedom Through Faith Ministries, PO Box 4936, Middle River, MD 21220.

ISBN-13: 978-0615483993

ISBN-10: 0615483992

This book is dedicated to my wife of 33 years (as of this writing). She has prayed for me, put up with me and stuck by my side even when I should have been kicked to the curb. She is the reason I have been able to answer the call of God on my life. She is my reason for living each and every day...

to be a Blessing to her.

Shin, I dedicate this book to you. I love you and I always will.

Bob

I would also like to thank Brother Kenneth Copeland and Brother Jerry Savelle for their teachings over all these years. It is because of their uncompromising Faith that I have learned to take my stand in Faith...it is because of them, this ministry is experiencing the success it has had. I strive to serve the LORD, but I hold these two men of Faith up as examples of integrity and excellence in ministry.

And finally, I want to thank JESUS for saving me, forgiving me of all my sins and giving to me the gift of everlasting life.

4

CONTENTS

	INTRODUCTION	7
1	Misconceptions Being Taught as Gospel	13
2	The Curse	21
3	The Blessing	35
4	The Blessing and Covenant of Abraham	45
5	What Happened When You Were Saved	61
6	The Family of God	77
7	The Sower Sows the Word	87
8	Don't Mess with the Mafia	111
9	**7 Keys to Answered Prayer**	121
10	Conclusion	135
	Example Prayer of Petition for Finances	137
	Author and Ministry Information	143

6

7 Keys to Answered Prayer

Introduction

Have you ever wondered if God really "hears" your prayers? I mean, how many times have you prayed and wondered if you said the "right" thing? You have heard preachers say, "ask according to God's will." So, if you do not get the answer you are looking for, does that mean you asked "out of God's will?"

Can you go to God and ask Him to save your loved ones? What about healing? Is it possible to pray for healing? Will God answer your prayer? Can you ask God to Bless your finances? Will He Bless your finances? Is asking for money or prosperity "wrong?"

Why does it appear that others get their prayers answered, but you don't? Are they doing something different? Do they have "greater Faith" than you do? Does God love them more than He loves you?

This book is going to help you find the answer to these plaguing questions. I have found that God does answer prayer.

Sometimes, we just need a little help in seeing "how" He answers our prayers. Sometimes we need a little help in "formalizing" our prayers. That is not to say there is a specific formula that guarantees results. But, if we can get our thoughts lined up with God's Word, then that allows our Faith to activate. And when we activate our Faith in God's Word to do what it says....we are on our way to getting our prayers answered.

In November 2009, I was in attendance at the Kenneth Copeland Washington, DC Victory Campaign. Kenneth Copeland was teaching on a concept of prayer that just exploded on the inside of me. I have been using this teaching as the basis for ALL of my prayers since then...and have experienced profound breakthroughs in getting my prayers answered. I want to share these things with you through this book.

First of all, let me emphasize, that God is not a respecter of persons. What He does for one person, He will do for every person....we have His promise on that. So, why doesn't He answer the prayers of every person...? It is up to US to get our Faith "tuned into" His Word.

Let me explain it using this example. You have a radio sitting on your desk. It is turned off. You hear nothing over the radio. Does that mean there is NO radio station broadcasting? NO. It just means you do not have your radio turned on. Radio stations are continually broadcasting over the airwaves. Now, you turn your radio on. But all you get is static. Does this mean there are no radio stations broadcasting? NO. It just means you have to "tune" into a station to hear the broadcast. If you tune into a station that is broadcasting "Rock" and you wanted to hear "Country and Western," you will be disappointed. You MUST tune into the station you want to hear.

Do you listen to "Rock" and "Country and Western" at the same time and on the same station? NO. Each station has a particular "band width" they are broadcasting on. You must "tune" into the appropriate "band width" in order to hear what you desire to listen to.

The same thing happens with God. God is here, talking to us through His Holy Spirit, all of the time. We just have to "tune in" to what He is saying. If we leave our spiritual "ears" turned off – we miss what He is telling us to do in order to be Blessed.

If we are listening to the devil or the world instead of listening to God, we miss what He is telling us to do. We are tuned into the wrong station!

How can we be sure we are listening to God? How can we KNOW He hears our prayers? Keep reading – I am about to take you through what I consider to be one of the most profound teachings on getting our prayers answered that you have ever heard. I believe, with all of my heart and soul, that this teaching will "tune you into" God. And, we have the promise of God, that if "we know He hears us, then we know we have the petitions we desire of Him."

12

Chapter 1

Misconceptions Being Taught as Gospel

Let's get something straight right from the beginning. Despite what you may have been taught by well meaning Christian people, God is FOR you and NOT against you! So many people for far too long have been taught wrong. I had heard from as far back as I can remember that God was out to "get you" if you messed up! That is totally, one hundred percent opposite the truth!

Where money is concerned, Christians have been taught that poverty is God's way of humbling us. That people in the ministry have taken a "vow of poverty." That if preachers do "get" anything, they have to give it away. We have been taught that Jesus was so poor, he did not even have a home to live in (Luke 9:58 *"Foxes have holes, and birds of the air have nests; but the Son of Man has nowhere to lay his head"*).

Jesus came to show us how to be Blessed! Poverty is under the curse! Jesus came to fulfill the Abrahamic Covenant. Abraham was RICH! Job was RICH! David was RICH! Solomon was RICH!

So why would Jesus be poor? And, if he was so poor, why did he have a treasurer? A poor man does not need a treasurer – a RICH man does!

Judas must have been giving A LOT of money AWAY! Because at the last supper, when Jesus told him to "do what you need to do," Judas got up and left. The other disciples thought he was going out to "give money to the poor." So he must have done that so often that the other disciples did not pay much attention to him leaving. This was after Jesus told them that one of the disciples was a traitor! So any unusual actions by any disciple would have raised immediate suspicion. But Judas' departure was just a natural part of their dinners, the other disciples did not think it was odd!

Christians have been taught for so long that "money is the root of all evil." But the scriptures do not say that. "The *love of money* is the root of all evil." (1 Timothy 6:10).

It costs money to preach the gospel. Just ask your Pastor the next time you see him! If you are not on the church Board of Directors and just think you can show up and all is well…and you give your little offering thinking "others" will give and that you need the money more than the church does…you are WRONG!

Granted, God will make sure that ministries which are doing God's work will be taken care of. But, the responsibility falls to us! God holds each of us responsible.

We have been taught that God allows sickness, disease or calamities to happen in our lives in order to "teach" us something. That is not scriptural. Sickness, disease and calamities are covered under the curses – and we have been redeemed from the curses! (Galatian 3:13-14).

We have been taught that our children ran from God because of something we have done in our past. We have been taught that our children must "find their own way." Both of these concepts are not scriptural. It is our responsibility as parents to pray for our children and teach them that God loves them and is there for them when we cannot be.

We have been taught that women need to be "submissive" in marriage and that the man is the "head of the house." We have been told that was in the Bible and therefore it must be so! We have been taught there is no option for divorce, even in an abusive marriage. But God does not want any of his children to be abused! And if there is abuse, obviously, the abuser is not saved nor acting in the image of God!

And in cases like that, the Bible says the child of God does not have to stay in the marriage! (1 Corinthians 7:15).

We have been taught that we can "never know what God will do." But the Bible says the Holy Spirit will show us all things! (John 14:25-27).

We have been taught that sometimes God answers our prayers and sometimes he doesn't. But the Bible says God's answers to our prayers are YES and AMEN. (2 Corinthians 1:20).

We have been taught that tithing went out with the Old Testament. That tithing is not something we have to do under the New Testament. But God says when you do not pay your tithes, you are stealing from Him! And it is the ONLY scripture in the Bible where God says you can "test" Him to see if He will answer your prayers! (Malachi 3:10).

We have been taught that speaking in "tongues" is not for today. That this spiritual gift went out with the Apostles. But that is not what the scriptures say. By praying in other tongues, we are able to communicate in God's language.

It is the Holy Spirit talking with our Spirit on a level that the devil cannot comprehend what is being said. It is a privilege only provided to born again believers! It is not to be abused. And it is a source of great power! (Mark 16:17).

We have been taught that miracle healings are not for today. That God developed medical centers and modern medicine so we would not have to rely on miracle healings. The question I have for you is this...Who gave the medical doctors the wisdom to develop the techniques and medicines to treat the condition? A medical healing or miracle is not something we should "seek" instead of utilizing the medical technology which is available. However, if medical technology is not able to treat the condition, don't shut God out of the picture! If you believe you will NOT receive a miracle – your prayer will be answered just as you believe! If you believe God is able...then He will!!!

The title of this book is "7 Keys to Answered Prayer." But, I do not want you to think there is a secret "formula" or a "Seven Step Program" which, if you follow, will get you the results you are looking for. This book is not designed to do that.

The purpose for this book is to develop in you the Faith in God to believe the prayers you are presenting to God WILL BE ANSWERED. (1John 5:14-15). There is no secret ritual or formula; you cannot "trick" God into answering your prayers; you cannot "buy" your answers.

You must operate by FAITH. Faith in God. Faith in Jesus. Faith in the Word. This book has been written to give you the foundation to present your prayers to God, knowing that He will answer them. Knowing that your Faith is what activates the Word in your life. Knowing that Jesus is the Word of God who was made flesh. Knowing that Jesus is always making intercession for you before God in order to get your prayers answered. Knowing that God will honor Jesus requests. Knowing that you are "justified" in God's eyes by what Jesus did for you on the cross.

Knowing that the "Just shall live by Faith."
(Habakkuk 2:4; Romans 1:17; Galatians 3:11; Hebrews 10:38).

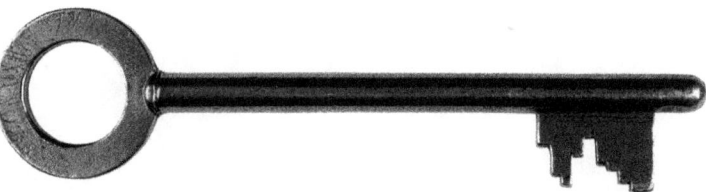

20

Chapter Two
The Curse

Before we can understand what God considers the Blessing that will answer prayer in our lives, we should look to see what REALLY is happening according to some of the teachings we have heard.

Deuteronomy 28:15 – 48 (The Curse).

15But it shall come to pass, if thou wilt not hearken unto the voice of the LORD thy God, to observe to do all his commandments and his statutes which I command thee this day; that all these curses shall come upon thee, and overtake thee:

16Cursed shalt thou be in the city, and cursed shalt thou be in the field. 17Cursed shall be thy basket and thy store. 18Cursed shall be the fruit of thy body, and the fruit of thy land, the increase of thy kine, and the flocks of thy sheep. 19Cursed shalt thou be when thou comest in, and cursed shalt thou be when thou goest out.

20The LORD shall send upon thee cursing, vexation, and rebuke, in all that thou settest thine hand unto for to do, until thou be destroyed, and until thou perish quickly; because of the wickedness of thy doings, whereby thou hast forsaken me.

21The LORD shall make the pestilence cleave unto thee, until he have consumed thee from off the land, whither thou goest to possess it. 22The LORD shall smite thee with a consumption, and with a fever, and with an inflammation, and with an extreme burning, and with the sword, and with blasting, and with mildew; and they shall pursue thee until thou perish.

23And thy heaven that is over thy head shall be brass, and the earth that is under thee shall be iron. 24The LORD shall make the rain of thy land powder and dust: from heaven shall it come down upon thee, until thou be destroyed.

25The LORD shall cause thee to be smitten before thine enemies: thou shalt go out one way against them, and flee seven ways before them: and shalt be removed into all the kingdoms of the earth.

26 And thy carcass shall be meat unto all fowls of the air, and unto the beasts of the earth, and no man shall fray them away. 27The LORD will smite thee with the botch of Egypt, and with the emerods (boils), and with the scab, and with the itch, whereof thou canst not be healed.

28The LORD shall smite thee with madness, and blindness, and astonishment of heart (or heart disease):

29And thou shalt grope at noonday, as the blind gropeth in darkness, and thou shalt not prosper in thy ways: and thou shalt be only oppressed and spoiled evermore, and no man shall save thee. 30Thou shalt betroth a wife, and another man shall lie with her: thou shalt build an house, and thou shalt not dwell therein: thou shalt plant a vineyard, and shalt not gather the grapes thereof.

31Thine ox shall be slain before thine eyes, and thou shalt not eat thereof: thine ass shall be violently taken away from before thy face, and shall not be restored to thee: thy sheep shall be given unto thine enemies, and thou shalt have none to rescue them.

32Thy sons and thy daughters shall be given unto another people, and thine eyes shall look, and fail with longing for them all the day long; and there shall be no might in thine hand. 33The fruit of thy land, and all thy labours, shall a nation which thou knowest not eat up; and thou shalt be only oppressed and crushed always:

34So that thou shalt be mad for the sight of thine eyes which thou shalt see. 35The LORD shall smite thee in the knees, and in the legs, with a sore botch that cannot be healed, from the sole of thy foot unto the top of thy head.

36The LORD shall bring thee, and thy king which thou shalt set over thee, unto a nation which neither thou nor thy fathers have known; and there shalt thou serve other gods, wood and stone. 37And thou shalt become an astonishment, a proverb, and a byword, among all nations whither the LORD shall lead thee.

38Thou shalt carry much seed out into the field, and shalt gather but little in; for the locust shall consume it. 39Thou shalt plant vineyards, and dress them, but shalt neither drink of the wine, nor gather the grapes; for the worms shall eat them.

40Thou shalt have olive trees throughout all thy coasts, but thou shalt not anoint thyself with the oil; for thine olive shall cast his fruit. 41Thou shalt beget sons and daughters, but thou shalt not enjoy them; for they shall go into captivity.

42All thy trees and fruit of thy land shall the locust consume. 43The stranger that is within thee shall get up above thee very high; and thou shalt come down very low. 44He shall lend to thee, and thou shalt not lend to him: he shall be the head, and thou shalt be the tail.

45Moreover all these curses shall come upon thee, and shall pursue thee, and overtake thee, till thou be destroyed; because thou hearkenedst not unto the voice of the LORD thy God, to keep his commandments and his statutes which he commanded thee:

46And they shall be upon thee for a sign and for a wonder, and upon thy seed for ever. 47Because thou servedst not the LORD thy God with joyfulness, and with gladness of heart, for the abundance of all things;

48Therefore shalt thou serve thine enemies which the LORD shall send against thee, in hunger, and in thirst, and in nakedness, and in want of all   things: and he shall put a yoke of iron upon thy neck, until he have destroyed thee.

In the first few versus, God is telling us if we will not listen to Him (how do we do that? God talks to us through His Word. So to "hear" God, we need to study and read His Word), then this is what will happen....

But it shall come to pass, if thou wilt not hearken unto the voice of the LORD thy God, to observe to do all his commandments and his statutes which I command thee this day; that all these curses shall come upon thee, and overtake thee: Cursed shall thou be in the city, and cursed thou shall be in the field. Cursed shall be thy basket and thy store. Cursed shall be the fruit of thy body, and the fruit of thy land, the increase of thy kine, and the flocks of thy sheep. Cursed shalt thou be when thou comest in, and cursed shalt thou be when thou goest out.

These versus tell us right away, something is wrong....WE are not doing something God has told us to do (listening to Him and doing what He instructs us to do). When we do not do what God says, then the curses "come upon us and overtake us." This means we cannot run fast enough to get away from them. They are so quick and overpowering, we cannot escape them.

We are cursed in the city or in the field (in other words, it does not matter where you live or try to move to).

Our "basket and store" are cursed. In today's society, we could say this is our "checking and savings accounts." Cursed is the fruit of our body, the fruit of our land, the increase of our kine and flocks of our sheep (these are considered "possessions" in the Old Testament. So the curse affects anything and everything we possess, including our children [fruit of our body]). In addition, the curse is operating in our lives every time we come into our house and every time we go out. That pretty much covers every aspect of our daily lives, don't you agree?

It does not matter where we live or try to move to ("If only I can get out of this city and move to another state…"). It does not matter if we try to stay at home or go to work (coming in and going out). Our children are under the curse because WE are under the curse (fruit of our body). Or possessions are under the curse. Our checking and savings accounts are under the curse. This does not sound good. But wait....it gets WORSE!

The LORD shall send upon thee cursing, vexation, and rebuke, in all that thou settest thine hand unto for to do, until thou be destroyed, and until thou perish quickly; because of the wickedness of thy doings, whereby thou hast forsaken me.

The LORD shall make the pestilence cleave unto thee, until he have consumed thee from off the land, whither thou goest to possess it. The LORD shall smite thee with a consumption, and with a fever, and with an inflammation, and with an extreme burning, and with the sword, and with blasting, and with mildew; and they shall pursue thee until thou perish. And thy heaven that is over thy head shall be brass, and the earth that is under thee shall be iron. The LORD shall make the rain of thy land powder and dust: from heaven shall it come down upon thee, until thou be destroyed.

God is not going to "send" curses on us...what He is doing is "allowing" the curses to come on us! In actuality, WE are allowing the curses to come upon us. After all, if we are not doing what He said to do...we must be following the devil's voice...and, reaping what is meant for him!

If this is happening, then everything you set your hand to do is under the curse! Diseases are clinging to your body and doctors can't get rid of the disease! Your prayers are not being answered because it seems like they are bouncing off of Heaven like you would bounce a ball off a wall…the earth is not providing resources for you, as if you plant a garden on a field of iron! On the areas you sow, instead of nurturing rain, you get a dust storm…and it continues until you are DESTROYED!

That sounds pretty bad, doesn't it? Guess what? It gets WORSE!

Your enemies will smite you at will (that means anyone who wants to do you harm – financially, professionally, whatever…can do so without fear of repercussions). It is enough that it could actually drive you insane. You will develop health conditions such as heart problems, vision problems, etc. You will grope around, trying to find a way out of your problems (like a blind man searching for something), but you will not prosper. You will be oppressed on every side and nobody can save you.

If you are married, your spouse will run off and have an affair with someone else and will not return to you. If you own a home, you lose it. If you have a business, you lose it.

Your possessions are taken from you (your car is repossessed). All of your assets are repossessed and auctioned off to cover your debts. You have absolutely nothing!

Well, Brother Bob, at least I have my family....

32 Thy sons and thy daughters shall be given unto another people, and thine eyes shall look, and fail with longing for them all the day long; and there shall be no might in thine hand.

The devil takes your children away from you, too. They either run away or...worse. And there is nothing you are able to do to save them. That is true destruction!

If you work, your job goes overseas. If you own a business, a foreign company becomes your competition and drives you bankrupt.

Thou shalt carry much seed out into the field, and shalt gather but little in; for the locust shall consume it. Thou shalt plant vineyards, and dress them, but shalt neither drink of the wine, nor gather the grapes; for the worms shall eat them. Thou shalt have olive trees throughout all thy coasts, but thou shalt not anoint thyself with the oil; for thine olive shall cast his fruit. Thou shalt beget sons and daughters, but thou shalt not enjoy them; for they shall go into captivity.

All thy trees and fruit of thy land shall the locust consume. The stranger that is within thee shall get up above thee very high; and thou shalt come down very low. He shall lend to thee, and thou shalt not lend to him: he shall be the head, and thou shalt be the tail.

When you try to keep your business going, or you try to "make ends meet" in your personal finances, you spend more than you are taking in.

You try and try and somebody else profits from your efforts. Your children go without, and all they learn is how to "survive" while in debt. That is the legacy you are teaching them. Eventually, you (and your children) are satisfied to live "in debt" forever.

Have you ever heard someone say, "Well, you might as realize now, you will always have bills. The sooner you realize that, the better off you will be."? Have you ever heard that? I have. And even though I had a lot of bills (and I am still working on them…), I know in the deepest part of my spirit man, that it just is not supposed to be that way!

But, if you continue to think and live like debt is "natural," you will always be the tail and not the head! "Well, Brother

Bob, it's not that bad. I have a few bills, but with my job, I can make it ok." Is that right?! Ok, do me a favor....call work tomorrow and tell them God is sending you to Mexico or Africa or even to stay at home and be a prayer warrior. Tell them you will be back when God tells you it is ok to come back to work. It might be a week, it might be a year...but, when God tells you, you will let them know.

What do you think their response will be? They will probably tell you to get your butt into work and stop talking so foolish! Will you quit? Probably not. Do you want to know why? Because you NEED the money which that job provides! "Well, Brother Bob, I do have a mortgage that has to be paid." So, you are the TAIL and not the HEAD!

To sum it all up, God says:

Moreover all these curses shall come upon thee, and shall pursue thee, and overtake thee, till thou be destroyed; because thou hearkenedst not unto the voice of the LORD thy God, to keep his commandments and his statutes which he commanded thee: And they shall be upon thee for a sign and for a wonder, and upon thy seed for ever. Because thou servedst not the LORD thy God with joyfulness, and with gladness of heart, for the abundance of all hings; Therefore shalt thou serve thine enemies which the LORD shall send against thee, in hunger, and in thirst, and in nakedness, and in want of all things: and he shall put a yoke of iron upon thy neck, until he have destroyed thee.

The reason all of this has happened to you: Because you would not listen to what God has instructed you to do. This is especially true concerning finances, but it can relate to health issues, family issues, relationship issues – whatever issue you want to bring up! If you don't do what God says to do, you open yourself up to the curses.

And, if you just go through the motions – you are still cursed! Because you are not serving God with a cheerful heart! And, as we already discussed, if you are not serving God, you ARE serving the devil and you will reap the devil's reward. And the devil will keep you under the curse until you are finally DESTROYED.

Now, I cannot finish this chapter allowing the devil to win! I want you to understand that everything we just talked about in this chapter is what happens when you DO NOT serve God and do so cheerfully. It allows the devil to destroy you. But, be of good cheer....Jesus has ALREADY defeated the devil!

The thief cometh not, but for to steal, and to kill, and to destroy: I am come that they might have life, and that they might have it more abundantly. (John 10:10).

These things I have spoken unto you, that in me ye might have peace. In the world ye shall have tribulation: but be of good cheer; I have overcome the world. (John 16:33)

The devil's purpose is to destroy you...to keep you under the curse. Why? So you will not be of any use to God. But, Jesus, in defeating the devil, has made a way for us to escape the curse and live under the Blessings (which we will see about next). Jesus Himself tells us not to be discouraged when we "fail" or "fall short." If we are quick to repent and confess our sins, we can continue living under the Blessings.

Jesus tell us to "be of good cheer" (to keep a cheerful attitude while we serve God, despite what the circumstances look like), because He has already overcome the world!

Chapter Three

The Blessing

Again, we go to Deuteronomy 28 to see what is in the Blessing God bestowed upon Israel – if they will listen to His voice and do what He says. In verses 1-14 we see the Blessing of God (which is for us).

1And it shall come to pass, if thou shalt hearken diligently unto the voice of the LORD thy God, to observe and to do all his commandments which I command thee this day, that the LORD thy God will set thee on high above all nations of the earth:

2And all these blessings shall come on thee, and overtake thee, if thou shalt hearken unto the voice of the LORD thy God.

3Blessed shalt thou be in the city, and blessed shalt thou be in the field.

4Blessed shall be the fruit of thy body, and the fruit of thy ground, and the fruit of thy cattle, the increase of thy kine, and the flocks of thy sheep.

5Blessed shall be thy basket and thy store.

6Blessed shalt thou be when thou comest in, and blessed shalt thou be when thou goest out.

7The LORD shall cause thine enemies that rise up against thee to be smitten before thy face: they shall come out against thee one way, and flee before thee seven ways.

8The LORD shall command the blessing upon thee in thy storehouses, and in all that thou settest thine hand unto; and he shall bless thee in the land which the LORD thy God giveth thee.

9The LORD shall establish thee an holy people unto himself, as he hath sworn unto thee, if thou shalt keep the commandments of the LORD thy God, and walk in his ways.

10And all people of the earth shall see that thou art called by the name of the LORD; and they shall be afraid of thee.

11And the LORD shall make thee plenteous in goods, in the fruit of thy body, and in the fruit of thy cattle, and in the fruit of thy ground, in the land which the LORD swore unto thy fathers to give thee.

12The LORD shall open unto thee his good treasure, the heaven to give the rain unto thy land in his season, and to bless all the work of thine hand: and thou shalt lend unto many nations, and thou shalt not borrow.

13And the LORD shall make thee the head, and not the tail; and thou shalt be above only, and thou shalt not be beneath; if that thou hearken unto the commandments of the LORD thy God, which I command thee this day, to observe and to do them:

14And thou shalt not go aside from any of the words which I command thee this day, to the right hand, or to the left, to go after other gods to serve them.

So, everything that we do is under the Blessing! Let's look at this a little closer, just like we looked at the curse. The Blessing of God belongs to US. It belongs to us NOW. How will we know what belongs to us if we do not study it?

1And it shall come to pass, if thou shalt hearken diligently unto the voice of the LORD thy God, to observe and to do all his commandments which I command thee this day, that the LORD thy God will set thee on high above all nations of the earth: 2And all these blessings shall come on thee, and overtake thee, if thou shalt hearken unto the voice of the LORD thy God.

If we will listen to what God is telling us to do, and then DO what He tells us to do…God will set us above everyone we come in contact with and the Blessings will overtake us and be evident in our lives. Now, this does not mean we will be "rulers" or "bosses" in every aspect of our lives. When God's

Blessings "come upon us and overtake us," that means no matter how fast we are going, the Blessings are faster than we are!

Have you ever been in a foot race and you were in the lead, but somebody who is faster catches up with you and then passes you? You were "overtaken." God's Blessings are "overtaking us" just like that! We cannot out run God's Blessings!

This means we will have God's FAVOR working in our lives. So, even if we are working as a janitor or an executive, who ever we have dealings with will look upon us with favor and we will be elevated in their eyes.

3Blessed shalt thou be in the city, and blessed shalt thou be in the field. 4Blessed shall be the fruit of thy body, and the fruit of thy ground, and the fruit of thy cattle, the increase of thy kine, and the flocks of thy sheep. 5Blessed shall be thy basket and thy store. 6Blessed shalt thou be when thou comest in, and blessed shalt thou be when thou goest out.

Blessed in the city and in the field. This means wherever we go, we are Blessed and the Blessing is working in our lives.

The fruit of our body (our children) are Blessed. God's Blessing is being extended to them because of US.

If you want to make sure your children are being protected and taken care of, even if you are not around, you need God's Blessing upon them...and YOU are responsible for making sure it happens (by listening to God's voice and doing what He tells you to do).

The fruit of your ground is Blessed. This is where you are sowing you seed to produce further harvests! Included is your tithes and offerings into other ministries. But it also includes investments you are making to further your business as well! The fruit of your cattle, the increase of your kine and the flocks of your sheep, again, talk about your possessions. You will be able to drive your car longer and will not have as many breakdowns. Everything you own will last longer and be more efficient (saving you money in the process – now that is a Blessing)!

You bank accounts and investment accounts are Blessed! You will know which investments to make, even in a down economy! Be sure to listen to God's voice, though. If you do...you will Prosper! If he says, SELL, you sell, even if it does not look like you should (think ENRON). If he says BUY, you buy, even if you don't think you should (think GOOGLE!).

But, how will you know His voice if you are not listening to Him constantly through His Word? You have to be tuned into God's Word and that only comes through spending time with Him (by studying His Word).

Blessed we are as we come into our house and Blessed we are when we go out. It does not matter where we are at – coming or going – the Blessing is working!!!

7The LORD shall cause thine enemies that rise up against thee to be smitten before thy face: they shall come out against thee one way, and flee before thee seven ways.

If anyone tries to establish a plan to bring us down (business or personal), it will be revealed to us so we can stop it. We also have God's promise to line things up in our behalf so their plans come to nothing in our lives (and will also be turned back onto their own heads in the process – making them look foolish for even trying such a stunt)!

8The LORD shall command the blessing upon thee in thy storehouses, and in all that thou settest thine hand unto; and he shall bless thee in the land which the LORD thy God giveth thee.

9The LORD shall establish thee an holy people unto himself, as he hath sworn unto thee, if thou shalt keep the commandments of the LORD thy God, and walk in his ways. 10And all people of the earth shall see that thou art called by the name of the LORD; and they shall be afraid of thee.

This means our bank accounts and investments accounts are Blessed. Our jobs are Blessed. If God tells us to "go over here and work" then that is where our Blessing is. If we follow His guidance, the Blessing is already there! You may say you want to move from Maryland to Texas (for example). But, if you do it because that is what "you want to do" and not because God tells you to go there, you will miss the Blessing. If you go because God says to go, you will be in the Blessing. If you don't go when God tells you to go, you miss your Blessing because your Blessing is waiting for you in Texas!

But, when you are where God tells you to be...and you are doing what God tells you to do...and you are listening to God continually – your Blessing is evident for everyone to see and they will all say, "God is surely Blessing him!" To be "afraid of thee" simply means they have respect for you (because of the Blessing).

11And the LORD shall make thee plenteous in goods, in the fruit of thy body, and in the fruit of thy cattle, and in the fruit of thy ground, in the land which the LORD swore unto thy fathers to give thee. 12The LORD shall open unto thee his good treasure, the heaven to give the rain unto thy land in his season, and to bless all the work of thine hand: and thou shalt lend unto many nations, and thou shalt not borrow.

And when we are where we are supposed to be, doing what we are supposed to do, and keeping our spiritual ears tuned into God's voice (through the study of His Word and spending time in prayer), then everything is under the Blessing! And God promises He will open the windows of Heaven and give us provision from His treasures (and I can assure you, there is no shortage in His treasures!). He will make sure we get rain on our fields (this was given to farmers in an agricultural setting. In modern times, it means what ever our jobs or investments are, the nurturing forces they need for growth will be provided by Him, in the proper timing for maximum growth!).

God will Bless ALL the work of our hands. Everything we

touch and do is under the Blessing! We will be so prosperous, we can lend to those that need help and we SHALL NOT BORROW!

This is absolutely part of the Blessing. As a matter of fact, I would venture to say this is THE MOST IMPORTANT PART OF OUR BLESSING!!! Never borrowing another dime as long you live! That is what I call THE BLESSING!

13And the LORD shall make thee the head, and not the tail; and thou shalt be above only, and thou shalt not be beneath; if that thou hearken unto the commandments of the LORD thy God, which I command thee this day, to observe and to do them: 14And thou shalt not go aside from any of the words which I command thee this day, to the right hand, or to the left, to go after other gods to serve them.

We will be made the head and not the tail. This means we are in charge of our own destiny, not subject to the whims of this world. We are above only and not beneath. This means we are above all circumstances that confront us. We do not have to bow the knee to the financial institutions of this world any longer. We do not have to go with hat in hand to the banker asking for mercy in obtaining a loan! We might just end up "owning the bank," Praise God!!! But it only happens if we stay "tuned into" God!

Chapter Four

The Blessing and Covenant of Abraham

The Blessing of Abraham. What does that have to do with us? What does the Blessing of Abraham have to do with the Blessing Moses talked about? And the Blessing we just studied, is that part of our lives? In Galatians 3:13-14, we see we have been *"redeemed from the curse because Jesus was made a curse for us... so that the Blessing of Abraham might come upon us through Jesus Christ our Lord so we might receive the promise of the Spirit through Faith."*

What does that mean? How does the Abrahamic Covenant and the Blessing of Jesus relate to us today?

First, let's look at the setting in the life of Abraham. Abraham was led by God to leave his home and land, taking his wife and settling in a land " which God will show him." He had no idea where he was going. All he knew was he was leaving his comfort zone. He did not have a home, he was going to live out of a tent. But, he believed God was leading him, so he left. He took his possessions, his wife and also took along his nephew, Lot (whom God did not tell him to take – so we have an example of how human reasoning interferes with God's plans. Lot would later end up as a headache for Abraham).

When Abraham came into the land God had promised him, he prospered! He was one of the richest men around! So much so that he and Lot ended up having to live apart! Abraham told Lot, "look, we have too much stuff. Pick which way you want to go and I will take the other way. There is no need in our off spring fighting each other over this land. You pick, I give you the choice." (*Authors paraphrase*). Lot looked out and chose what he thought would be a good choice – the land of Sodom.

As soon as Lot packed up and left, God appeared to Abraham and told him to walk through the land, God was going to Bless him everywhere he walked. Why did God wait until Lot left….Because God originally told Abraham to "leave his family and follow Him." When Abraham took Lot with him, he was going against what God told him to do! Once he came to the realization that Lot had to leave (and Lot left), he was back into the Blessing of God! Notice though, that the Blessing was still active in Abrahams life because he was "rich" even in that setting! He just was unable to "tune in" to God to get further directions!

Abraham was getting so rich, he was worried that the people around him would try to kill him to get his "stuff" including Sari his wife. So he devised a scheme where if anyone asked, she would say she was Abraham's sister. This almost cost him twice with local kings. Finally, he admitted she was his wife and the Blessing of God worked in his behalf and protected him from the local kings.

God then appeared to Abraham and told him that he and Sari were going to have a child. Up to now, Abraham was known as Abram. But God told him to change his name to Abraham – Father of many nations. Abraham began to go around introducing himself to others by saying, "Hello. My name is Father of Many Nations...how are you?" This sounded strange to everyone, but what was he doing? He was calling his circumstances as being subject to God's will...he was saying things that were not currently in existence as if they already were done! (Hebrews 11:1) That is speaking by Faith!

When God told him and Sari (whom God changed her name to Sarah), Abraham was 76 years old and Sarah was 66. Now, without being too graphic here, this was not going to be an immaculate conception.

Sarah and Abraham were going to have to work at having this baby of promise. Eventually, they grew tired of "trying," and Sarah devised a plan to "help" God out. This became Ishmael. And that "helping" is still haunting Israel today.

After Ishmael was born, 13 more years elapsed before God spoke to Abraham again. When He did, Abraham was ready to listen! But, when God said, "Next year, your son of promise, through Sarah, will be here," Abraham started to laugh (and so did Sarah). They just could not fathom how God was going to that. Abraham was almost 100 years old and Sarah was 90. There was absolutely no way they could wrap their little feeble old minds around how God was going to do that. But, obviously, they "tried" to have a baby at least one more time – because Sarah ended up pregnant!!! Don't you know that was the talk of the town!!!

That is a short explanation of what happened to Abraham. But, how did he get his Faith to such a high level of belief? What happened to convince Abram (Abraham) that God would do what God promised to do? It started with the cutting of the Covenant. Let's look at what that actually means…because it is vital to our understanding of the Blessing that is at work in our life today.

Let's start with the Covenant HESED.

It is a driving compassion to give. To enter into a covenant forever, especially a blood covenant. It is a covenant you enter into for someone else's benefit. It is a promise to do something or to give something until it is too good to be true. Then you swear in your own blood (to your own hurt) to make it come to pass. That is how the person you enter into covenant with knows you are not lying. The seed of that kind of love from God is in us at the time we are born again!

The covenant of HESED is seen 242 times in the Old Covenant of the Bible. It is encompassed by loving kindness, grace, steadfast love, mercy, goodness, faithfulness, devotion, favor and strength.

A HESED type of covenant has been recorded in all ancient civilizations. It was how the ancient people survived. We have moved away from this type of relationship in our "modern" society, but a covenant is still here. We call it a "contract." Have you ever signed a contract? Then you entered a Covenant with who ever you were signing up with. Usually it is a contract to pay somebody – even to your hurt.

In the days of Abraham, families would cut covenant based upon strengths and weaknesses. Not on things in common. It was never entered into lightly. It was a serious negotiation. It was designed to continue beyond the current generation who was cutting the covenant (It would usually last at least eight generations). It was impossible to cancel the covenant without (somebody's) death. It was actually more binding than having the same mother! It was to be forever, whether the families would continue to get along or not!

A person would be hand selected to represent the tribe or family. A covenant site would be mutually chosen where everyone concerned would come to witness the cutting of the covenant. A sacrificial animal would be selected. The animal would be parted down the backbone, splitting it in half. It would be allowed to fall into two separate parts, creating a walk-way between the two halves, where the ground would be covered in blood between the halves.

Each man would then take off his coat and give it as a gift to the other family. The coat was a family recognition symbol. It stood for who the family was and represented the "authority" of the person who was giving it.

He was saying, "I give myself and my authority to you." Each person would then exchange weapons. In effect saying, "I give my strength to you. Your enemies are now my enemies. Even if I die, I will stand with you in battle." Each person would then walk through the blood trail, twice! They would stop in the middle and say something to the effect of "Even as this animal has died, I will stand with you, even in the midst of death." By standing in the blood, it represented promises that could not be broken. These promises were made by each family representative out loud, to all who were present. These promises were the Blessings of the Covenant.

There would then be an exchange of cursing between the two representatives. It would be viscous and cruel. But it was meant to mean that if you break your promises, these are all the bad things, which will happen to you. It was graphic, but necessary. And, even if a favorite son was to break the covenant, it was the responsibility of the family to kill the son in order to keep the covenant in place. Otherwise, the curses would come upon both families.

This was very serious business. We have a hard time understanding these things today. But a very serious example is the so called "street gangs" that infect our cities today.

They are operating in a wicked, twisted form of this type of covenant. But to the members of the gangs, it is a blood covenant they take very seriously, even to the point of death if necessary. Now, I am not saying everyone should run out and join a gang. Heaven forbid. But I am using that as a type of example for what a Covenant is from the perspective of a Covenant minded culture, such as Abraham was living in.

Each representative made the promises, using God as a third party witness. There was then the cutting of the flesh by wrist or hand and an inter-mingling of blood. They would raise their hands in the air (in Praise to God) and show everyone that a new blood family is now in existence. I am not talking about a little nick with a knife and they can put a band-aid on it and let it heal. I am talking about a deep, penetrating cut down to bone. This type of cut would take weeks to heal and leave a huge scar on their hands. The scar would never go away…always representing and reminding them that they are in a covenant. Their blood was mingled together, running down each others arms and falling into and mixing with the blood of the sacrifice.

There is now a new family in existence. So there had to be a name change, too. They were one family now. There is a new relationship established – HESED!

If this covenant was made between a warrior and a farmer, the new family name might be Warrior-Farmer or Farmer-Warrior. But there was now a new relationship and a new family established in the land.

Usually, they would exchange daughters to be married to the other family's sons. This way, the off spring would automatically KNOW they were part of each others family! Their blood lines would be mixed together, just like they were between the representatives at the sacrifice, sealing the deal forever.

Then, after the ceremony, there was the Grand Finale – the covenant meal! The leaders would share a cup of wine. As they drank from the cup, they would state something to the effect of, "Drink my life's blood as I drink your life's blood. I see you fulfilling all the terms of the covenant as I help to fulfill your life." They would then feed each other a piece of bread signifying "take me, and all I have, for I am all yours."

How does this relate to Abraham? Abraham was the first person ever to seek God beyond his natural senses. His Faith was deep enough that God could speak to him and he would hear and understand. When God was speaking about the covenant to Abraham, it was called "preaching the Gospel" to him (Galatians 3:8). What is the Gospel? God was preaching GOOD NEWS to Abraham. What is the Good News? That God was now in covenant with Abraham!!! And Abraham was smart enough to know that a covenant can not be broken!!! Especially a Covenant with GOD, Creator of the Universe!!! Abraham was thinking, "I've got it made, now!"

When God made the promises of Blessing and offspring to Abraham, he asked God, "how can I know these things will be, since I am old and so is Sarah." It was a very good question…At that time, Abraham was planning on making his chief servant his heir!

So God responded in a way that Abraham was very familiar with - a Blood Covenant! It was so moving upon Abraham, that he would not even let the birds come down and land on the covenant pieces. And when he seen God's own foot prints in the blood, and heard the Blessing God pronounced, he knew that he knew that he knew, God could NEVER change His mind as long as Abraham walked according to the Covenant. If Abraham did what he was supposed to do, according to the Covenant – then he could hold God accountable to uphold His portion! Abraham thought to himself, "I have a covenant partner in God! He cannot lie. He cannot cheat me. He is the Creator of all life. He is the one who can create everything out of nothing! I cannot lose in this deal as long as I walk according to the Covenant He made with me. Whatever he asks me for, I am going to give it. Whatever He asks me to do, I will do. I will give Him anything and everything, knowing He will give me everything and anything!"

That is why, when God told him to sacrifice Isaac, Abraham did not hesitate. He did not know "how" God was going to do it, but he knew God had promised that, "through Isaac shall your seed be." Notice Abraham did not fret over what God asked him. The scripture does not say he went and discussed it with Sarah. It appears he did not even tell Sarah! He probably figured she would try to screw it up like she did with Ishmael! So, he went by Faith to offer Isaac as a sacrifice to God. He would not hold back anything from his Covenant with God. If God asked for it, it was his, including Isaac.

Notice when he went "to the place" where the sacrifice was going to take place, he did not discuss it with the men which were with him. He told the men, "You wait here. The boy and I will go over there and perform the sacrifice and "we" will return to you." He was already speaking by Faith! He knew God would have to do something miraculous, and he was going to be there to see it!

He was going to go through the entire sacrifice. We know that because even Isaac asked him, "here is the wood and the fire, but where is the lamb (the sacrifice)?" Now, at this time, it is estimated Isaac was probably in his late teens to early twenties. He was not this little five or six year old kid. And, we can infer from the question, that he had been taught about the Covenant! He knew what sacrificing to God meant. He knew what was required and what to do. And he knew you could not offer God a blemished sacrifice, it had to be THE BEST you had. That is why he asked the question.

He knew there were wild animals around there. But they were not "good enough" to offer as a sacrifice! But, what did Abraham respond with, "God will provide himself a lamb (for the sacrifice)." Prophetically, he was talking about Jesus, but in his mind, he was talking about then and now. (Genesis 22:7-9).

In his mind, Abraham believed he was going to bind Isaac, put him on the altar, kill him, dismember him and burn him (the reason for the wood and the fire). Then, he was going to sit back and wait on God. He was not going to return to those men alone. He was going to sit there and watch God reassemble those burnt ashes into the body of Isaac and then watch as Isaac came back to life. Abraham KNEW God could do it and he fully expected it to happen.

So when he had prepared everything and was ready to bind Isaac, notice the Bible does not say, "and a big fight erupted between the two." The next scripture does not say, "And they found Isaac two months later living in Egypt!" Isaac could have "taken the old man" if he wanted to! But he did not fight it. He knew the promises God had given to Abraham. He knew that "through Isaac" shall the seed of Abraham be called. He knew that God could not lie. He knew all the promises that God had already fulfilled for his dad. He knew God was going to use his sacrifice for something really special…and he wanted in on it, too!

He "willingly offered himself" as the sacrifice! (and that obligated Jesus to do the same!) We then see that God intervened once Abraham raised that knife and was ready to fulfill the sacrifice. This sacrificial act committed God Himself to the sacrifice of Jesus because of what Abraham had done.

But, that is the power of the Covenant. The Old Testament was a covenant of the Flesh. The New Covenant is a covenant of the inner man, which we will now look into also.

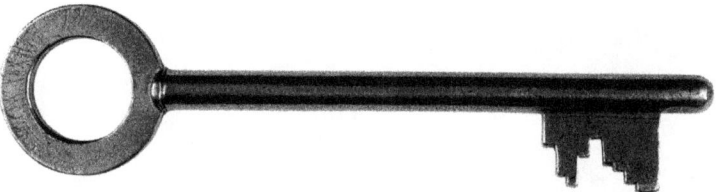

60

Chapter Five

What Happened When You Were Saved

Ok, this is where the rubber meets the road! If you are saved, you have the "Hope of Glory" dwelling inside of you. Which means you have Christ in you, the Holy Spirit of God Almighty living in you. Your spirit man died the day you made Jesus the Lord of your life!

In the natural, when a person dies, their spirit leaves their body. There is nothing left but a carcass. Think of it like this…if I had a pretty blue suit that I wore to every official gathering, you would see me far off and, even though you could not see my face clearly, you would identify the suit and say, "here comes brother Bob!" Now, what if I were to take that suit coat off and hang it on the back of a chair and walk away. You would not say, "Brother Bob is sitting over in that chair." No, you would say, "that's Brother Bob's suit coat, but he is not here." Because "I" am not inside the suit anymore. Without me, the suit cannot get up and walk around. It just "lays" there.

Our bodies are the same as that suit. Without our spirit man inside, it just lays there. Go to any funeral home and look inside the casket! The spirit man has left the body and the body is just laying there. That is what happens when a person dies...the spirit man inside leaves the body and the body begins to decompose. There is no "life" inside the body.

But, when you made Jesus the Lord of your life, when you made Him your Savior, He sent His Spirit – the Holy Spirit of God Himself, to "live" inside of you. YOU DIED at the exact moment you gave your life to Him! Just like He gave His life for YOU – you gave your life to HIM! It was a sacrifice on your part! WHAAATTTT!!!??? "Brother Bob, how could I sacrifice myself for Jesus? Didn't He sacrifice Himself for ME?" YES, YES, YES – a thousand times YES!!!! Don't you get it?????

Jesus "gave" Himself over to death on the cross in order to "give" you Eternal life. But, to get Eternal Life, you have to let Him, through the Holy Spirit, come and "live" inside of you. In order to do that, you have to give Him permission. He is not like the devil, who will force his way in, like a thief that he is. You have to invite Him inside. You must present your body as a place for Him to live…a Living Sacrifice on your part. (Romans 12:1).

Now, think back to basic science classes you attended in school. Matter cannot occupy the same space at the same time. If you fill a glass with water to the brim, put a lid on it and insert two straws and blow through one, water is forced up into the second straw. This is because you are blowing air into the container, which forces the water up and out of the other straw. Matter (air and water) cannot occupy the same space at the same time.

Your spirit, the one that was made of sin, conceived in sin, loved to sin and was 100% sin, cannot, will not nor could it ever, occupy the same space as the Holy Spirit of God. The Glory of God would "kill" the sinful man – immediately. Think back to the Temple and the Holy of Holy's in the Old Testament. Before the High Priest could enter the Inner Sanctum of God (and only ONCE per year could he go inside to offer sacrifice for the nation of Israel), he had to completely cleanse himself, spend a lot of time in prayer, offer sacrifice for "his" sins, then and only then approach the Ark of God.

He had tinkling bells on his garment, and some traditions say they would tie a rope around his ankle. If the people outside stopped hearing the tinkling bells, they would grab the rope and pull his body out (because they could not go inside).

If there was any unrepentant sin in his life, the Glory of God would kill it. Just being in the presence of God was enough for sin to die. And if his spirit was still sinful, his spirit would die in the presence of God!

So, just as matter cannot occupy the same space as other matter, your sinful spirit cannot occupy the same space as the Glory of God's Holy Spirit. So, the moment you asked Jesus to save you – HE DID! At that exact moment, He sent the Holy Spirit to live INSIDE YOU! At that EXACT moment, your spirit man – the sinful nature which "you" were made of – DIED! Just like when Jesus died on the cross!

Jesus' last Words were, "Father, into your hands, I commend my spirit,"(Luke 23:46). Your "last words" were something to the effect of "Jesus, I give my life to you" (that may not be exact, but close). The Bible then says, Jesus, "gave up the ghost," or HE DIED! Your body "gave up your ghost" at the exact moment Jesus came in to live within your body! The Glory of God came in and YOU DIED! You were re-created in the image of God Himself and His Spirit took up residence in your body!

That is why you are still able to walk around and function in your day-to-day existence. Just as if someone came and picked up my suit coat off of the back of that chair, put it on and started to walk around! It's not me inside of that suit anymore – it is the other person! The suit still looks the same, but it is not "me" inside. Someone may even say, "Is that Brother Bob? He looks different." They are looking at the suit, not ME!

Glory to God!!! I really pray you are getting this. It is fundamental to understand what happened at the moment you got saved in order to understand the HOW and WHY of getting the results to your prayers that you desire.

That is why, in Romans 4:18-24, Paul talks about how the faith of Abraham believed what God had promised him, and that God was able to perform the promises. Even when everything seemed to be against him, Abraham never lost his hope and held God accountable for fulfilling the promise He had made to Abraham.

He (Abraham) did not consider his own body (being a hundred years old) or Sarah's body (being 90 years old), Abraham did not stagger at the promise of God; but was STRONG IS HIS FAITH, (always) giving Glory to God, being fully persuaded that, what He had promised (to Abraham),

He (God) was able also to perform. And therefore "it" (Abraham's unyielding faith) was counted to him as righteousness. Now, it was not written for his sake (Abraham) alone, that it was imputed to him; But FOR US ALSO, to whom "it shall be imputed" (our unyielding faith), if WE believe on Him (God) that raised up Jesus our Lord from the dead."

Romans Chapter 6 talks about how we "died" with Jesus on the cross. We were "crucified" with Him and were also "raised up" with Him when God raised Jesus from the dead! Even though we were not "alive" at the time of the crucifixion, there is no time or space with God.

So, the moment Jesus "gave" His life on the cross and died, we are translated to that "exact moment" the second we "give" our life to Jesus. He takes upon Himself ALL of our sins.

And the exact moment God raised Jesus from the dead, we are immediately translated to that moment and, just as the Holy Spirit of God flooded back into Jesus' body and brought Him back to Life (never to die again - Romans 6:9), the Holy Spirit flooded into OUR body, giving immediate Life to our body and death has no more reign over us (Romans 6:11)!!! Glory to God!!!!

Now, the exact Law (of sin and death) which separated us from receiving from God, has been destroyed forever by the death and resurrection of Jesus – and by the death and resurrection of US by God's Holy Spirit. When the Spirit of God came in, the spirit of death and sin went out (just like the water in the container)! Praise be to God!!!

Romans 8:2 says, *"For the Law of the Spirit of life in Christ Jesus has made me free from the law of sin and death."* Verse 15-17 says, *"For you have not received the spirit of bondage "again" to fear; but you have received the Spirit of adoption, which is why we can cry 'Abba'* (or 'Daddy') – *Father* (calling out to God). *The Spirit* (of God Himself) *bears witness with our spirit* (or the Spirit living within us) *that we ARE the children of God; and if* (God's) *children, then we* (are also) *heirs; heirs of God, and joint heirs with Christ; if so be that we suffer(ed) with Him, that we may be also glorified together* (with Him).

Luke 15 talks about a parable Jesus taught, talking about (who we refer to as) the Prodigal Son. This son was a joint heir with his brother. He asked his father for his portion of his inheritance NOW. And it was given to him. He then squandered his inheritance by living a sinful lifestyle.

But, eventually, he came to his senses and realized, "I need my father. I may never be able to be restored into my place as his son and an heir, but at least I will have my needs met."

But, as the story continues to unfold, as he returns to his father's house, the father sees him "far off." This means that the father had to be "looking' for the son. He was constantly waiting for his lost son to return. He was looking, and looking, and looking – always believing that one day, he would come back. And then, one day – there he is! And the father, being old, still "runs to meet him."

And the father hugs him (pig stink and all!) and rejoices over his return. The father orders that a celebration take place because his son has returned home. Even before the son can basically throw himself on the father's mercy and give his speech that he has been rehearsing the entire trip home, his father has restored the son to full family standing.

He has the family clothes, the family shoes the family ring – everything! (Now, the other son had a problem with it, but that is a different sermon! I want you to see that when the sinful son returned home, the father restored him to a position of authority just as if he never left).

Now, I want to share something with you that I have read hundreds of times over the years, but only recently received a revelation about it. Notice, the father said to "kill the fatted calf," for his son had returned home. The oldest son was upset with the father, and said, "You never even gave me a "kid" (goat) and you gave him the "fatted calf."

I always assumed this was in reference to the "party" that the father wanted to have. But, think about this in Biblical terms concerning what we are studying – sin, sacrifice and the gift of everlasting life! Families in the day and age we are talking about concerning the Prodigal Son, would raise a calf for a special sacrifice once per year. This is when the offering for their sins would be forgiven and they would be "good to go" for another year. This "fatted calf" was for that purpose.

So, when the father gave the command to kill the "fatted calf," he was saying, in essence, to make the offering NOW for my son! All of his sins will be erased and forgiven and he will be restored to his rightful position in the family. KILL THE SACRIFICE!!!

This upset the brother…the father never just killed the sacrifice for him! Not even a goat! That is what the disagreement was about! That is why the father said, "You are with me always, and everything I have is yours. But, your brother was lost, now he is found. He has come home! We must make the sacrifice so his sins will be forgiven by God! This must be done NOW!"

This is an example of how we are restored to God's family. Yes, we messed up our lives. Yes, we sinned. Yes we deserve just punishment. But, God paid the price through Jesus. Jesus "gave" Himself in our behalf.

So, God commands that, when we "come to our senses and return to Him," that we be clothed with the family clothing (the garments of salvation), that we have the family shoes placed on our feet (feet shod with the preparation of the gospel of peace) and have the family ring placed on our fingers (sealed with the Holy Ghost – who now lives in us).
"Kill the sacrifice!!!" Jesus has already paid the price for our sins! Glory to God!!! We have been RESTORED to full family status! We are (again) JOINT HEIRS with Jesus!

That is what happened when you made Jesus the Lord of your life! As brother Kenneth Copeland says – "Shout AMEN, somebody!"

Now, we have already studied the curse (Deuteronomy 28:15-28). We have studied how debt, poverty, lack, sickness, disease, relationship problems, EVERYTHING is covered under the curse.

We have studied how we have been REDEEMED from the curse by the sacrifice of Jesus (read Galatians 3:13-14). We have studied how the faith of Abraham paved the way for us to be restored into right standing with God. We have studied how the Holy Spirit flooded into our bodies the moment we received Jesus as our Savior. We have studied how God restored us through adoption to be His children and how God has given us full family status again.

He (God) did this so we can live a Blessed life. We can live under the Blessing at all times. We have already studied the Blessing in the previous chapter. What I want to leave you with as we close this chapter is a summary of what happened and why – when Jesus gave Himself in sacrifice, and we accepted His sacrifice, the same Blessing that was on Abraham was able to come upon us.

In Galatians 2:20, Paul stated very plainly, *"I am crucified with Christ* (as we already studied): *nevertheless, I LIVE; yet* (it is) *not*

I (that lives), *but Christ* (who) *lives within me: and the life which I now live in the flesh, I live by the Faith of the Son of God, who loved me, and gave Himself for me."*

So, we live by Faith in that, what God promised would come upon us (Eternal Life), does so by the Death, Burial and Resurrection of Jesus. And that, what God promised, He is able also to perform.

In Galatians 3:8-9, 16, 26, and 29, we see it laid out for us.
"And the scripture, forseeing that God would justify the heathen (that's us before we were saved) *through Faith, preached before the* (written) *gospel unto Abraham, saying, 'In you shall all nations* (people) *be Blessed.' So then, they* (you) *which be of Faith* (in God fulfilling His promises) *are Blessed with* (the same Faith) *of Faithful Abraham. Now to Abraham and his seed* (descendants) *were the promises made. He* (God) *did not say seeds as of many; but as of one, and to the seed which is Christ. For you are all children of God by Faith in Christ Jesus. And, if you are Christ's then you are Abraham's seed* (descendants) *and heirs according to the promise* (made by God to Abraham)."

So, we see we are Blessed with the same Faith as Abraham used to become the "Father" of all Faithful people! And it is the same Faith that Jesus used to become our sacrifice. And it is the same Faith that God used to raise Jesus from the dead. And it is the same Faith the Holy Spirit used in order for Him to take up residence inside our bodies.

Galatians 3:13-14 states:

"Christ has redeemed us (paid the total price due) *from the curse of the law, being made a curse for us* (in our place): *for it is written, Cursed is everyone who is hung on a tree:* (So) *that the Blessing of Abraham might come on the Gentiles* (those that are separated from God) *through* (the Life) *of Jesus Christ; that we might receive the promise of the Spirit* (of God) *through Faith."*

So, we see how, through Jesus' death, burial and resurrection, we became adopted into the Family of God – by Faith, not by the Law. But, how does that help us? Does that mean I get to go to Heaven? How does that help me now? (As Rev. Kenneth Hagin said, "It is good to know we will be Blessed in the Sweet by and by, but what about the rotten here and now!?").

It is good to know that, when you die and depart from your natural, flesh body, that you will be going to Heaven. That is, absolutely, the best promise you can take away from spending time in this study and by spending time in the Word of God. If you do not get ANYTHING else – get SAVED!!! The short amount of time we spend on this earth is nothing when compared to all of eternity.

As a matter of fact – I would like you to say this simple prayer out loud. If there are other people around and you are a little shy or nervous, just say it out loud just enough for your own two ears to hear. If you have never asked Jesus to come into your life, this is YOUR moment. If you have asked Him to save you before, and you have drifted away (like the Prodigal son we just studied about), now is the time to come back home. Just say this simple prayer – and mean it with all you heart:

Jesus, I come before you today with all my heart, asking you to forgive me of ALL my sins. I have both, knowingly and unknowingly, sinned against you and against your Word. I have sinned my whole life and I am not worthy to stand before you or Father God on my own. I realize that. I ask you today, to forgive me. I ask you to look into my heart and see that what I am asking is true. I believe you died in my place on the cross, so many, many years ago.

But, I also believe, that when you were buried, I was buried. And when God spoke the Spirit of Life back into you, He also sends the same Spirit of Life into me RIGHT NOW. This same Power of God now gives to me the Holy Spirit of God to live on the inside of me forever more. It is now no longer me living on the inside, by myself, it is the Holy Spirit living in me! Thank you Jesus for saving me. Thank you for forgiving me of my sins and thank you for giving to me the Eternal Gift of Everlasting Life. Now, all that is yours is mine and all that is mine is now yours! In Jesus Holy Name I pray....Amen!

WELCOME TO THE FAMILY!!!

(Note from Brother Bob: "If you just prayed that prayer of Salvation, I want to rejoice with you. I have some materials I would like to send you, absolutely FREE. These materials will help you to begin your walk in your new, Christ based life. Just write me and let me know and I will get them out to you immediately – and I will pay the postage. Or, if you want, you can go to our website and send me an email: brotherbob@ftfm.org. Our address and contact information are on the website at www.ftfm.org, along with some other information that will Bless you.)

Chapter Six

The Family of God

So, just what does that mean – The Family of God? Well, first and foremost, it means you are never alone. The Holy Spirit has moved in! So no matter what evil you face, no matter what dire circumstances confront you, no matter what sickness you are facing, no matter how big the bill is – you are not alone!

And, as a member of the family, you have a Father who loves you very, very much. More than you will ever realize on this earth. He loved you so much, that when the devil was holding you ransom, God sent His only Beloved Son, Jesus, to rescue you. And it cost Jesus His life. He died, getting you set free. He died when He did not have to die. He died because He loved you, too. Do you see how precious you are in the sight of God?

This is a very poor example, but it will demonstrate the point I am trying to make here. For those of you that have more than one child (and for those that only have one child or for those who only have brothers / sister or just very good best friends), think of your relationship in this manner.

A very bad and evil person has kidnapped your son or daughter. You know where he / she is being kept, but you have no jurisdictional authority to go and get them. Not only that, but the police and government has told you there is nothing they can do, either. Their best advice to you is to just forget about them and move on with your life. Even though you have proof they are being tortured, hurt and being used in slave labor, you are told repeatedly there is nothing that can be done.

So, you develop a plan. You (if you are a woman) (your wife if you are a man) have another son. But, from a very young age, you begin to prepare him for a very specific rescue mission. He is trained in how to use weapons that the enemy has no access to. He is trained in counter espionage techniques. He is trained in hand to hand combat. He is trained in all manner of psychological warfare. He knows the manuals by heart and can quote chapter and verse. You move to and bring him up in the area and culture in which you plan to make your rescue.

When the time is right, you send him. Your only shot at winning your entire family back. But to do so, he must go right into the pit of the enemy's camp. But he goes willingly.

He knows he may have to give his life to get your child (his brother) out and set free. But he willingly gives himself for the cause.

During the course of the rescue mission, he is captured. He is executed. But the enemy caught him illegally. When the enemy killed him, it was an unlawful act! NOW the government has a reason to move in. They have the authority to not only rescue your lost child, but they secure the body of your son. They take all the possessions of the enemy, stripping him of everything. The enemy has no more authority to operate in any realm.

Anticipating that something may happen to your son on the rescue mission, you have made provision for medical treatment. The government has said "it is no use, he is dead." But swift actions on your part and the medical specialists you have put in place are able to keep him on life support. Within three days, he is able to be taken off life support and function on his own. Just 40 days later, he is able to return home to you.

You have now received your son back home. The child that has been rescued, you have now left in charge of the clean up operation in the land which held he/she captive. The Governing Authority has told your child that, if they need anything, to let you or them know. If anyone challenges your child's authority, they are to let you know. If anyone tries to take them prisoner again, they are to let you know. You and your son are awaiting your lost son's return home to be with you, just as soon as the clean up operation is completed.

That is a synopsis of what God has done for you. God and Jesus are waiting in Heaven, expecting His enemies to made into a footstool. They are expecting YOU to do so. You are in charge down here. You have the responsibility to let God know what you need in order to do your job. You are responsible to let God know if a little demon from hell is trying to disrupt the clean up operation.

That is what your job is here, now. That is a simplified version of what God and Jesus did for you. In no way do I limit God to just this simple outline. I give it just to try and let you see WHY God sent Jesus to rescue you. How God planned your rescue for a very long time. How Jesus was trained and knew what He had to do, up to and including giving His life for you. And how God already had a plan in place to bring Him back from the dead. How the devil overstepped his authority in killing Jesus, which turned all of creation away from him and back to JESUS! Praise God!!!

As a child of God, you have a Brother who is actually closer than a brother. You have a Father who has done everything in order to make sure your "every need is met, according to His riches in Glory – by Christ Jesus." (Philippians 4:19). Not some needs – EVERY NEED! That implies you have no needs left undone!

Nobody has ever brought a need before the Father and had Him look at Jesus and the Angels standing around and say, "We didn't see that one coming!" or "You're on your own with that one." NO...Jesus says we are complete in Him. Jesus says, "Ask and you shall receive." Jesus says we can approach the Throne of God BOLDLY. Jesus said when we "ask in Faith, believing, we shall receive." Jesus said, "Whatsoever thing you ask the Father, in my Name, He will give it to you." (John 14:14).

"So, Brother Bob," you might ask, "why is it I don't get all of my prayers answered? Why is it I keep asking for the same thing over and over, but do not see any results?"

Maybe you do not realize your status as a full-fledged member of the Family of God yet! Lets' look at this one more time before we get into some really good stuff on getting your prayers answered. You HAVE to understand this part of the Gospel in order for ANY of it to work!

In Genesis, after the fall of Adam, man had full understanding about how to use his words according to Faith. That is why God said, "They now know the difference between good and evil." (Genesis 3:22). This means man had an UNDERSTANDING of the difference. And since he had an understanding, he also had the ability to use what he understood. That is why in Genesis Chapter 11, when the Tower of Babel was being built, God had to put a stop to it. Let's go there and see...

There was only ONE language at the time....God's language. We would call it "Tongues" today. It was the language of the Holy Spirit. And, the people decided they did not need God anymore.

It says in verses 2-6, summarized, that "they found a plain and dwelt there. And they said, "Let US make brick."

(Now why did they want to make brick? God always had them make alters out of natural stones. Brick is man's attempt at making things perfect...each brick looks just like the next one. It is made out of a bunch of mud and formed and baked in an oven. Somebody has to make it [and that was the beginning of Socialism in the world...the government deciding what is best for the people and then "supervising" their work for the common good]. They decided "they" would build their own alter and tower and reach up into Heaven....they knew best and did not need God..).

So the people said, "Let US build...Let US make a city...Let US make a tower...Let US make a name for ourselves."

Then God came down and said, "they all have one language (which was His) and this thing they begin to do, nothing will be restrained from them, which they have IMAGINED to do." They can conceive it in their hearts, think of it with their minds and speak it out their mouths...and nothing shall be restrained from them...

So, God speaks one Word – BABBLE and the whole shooting match was over! Through Noah and on to Abram we go...We have already studied the Covenant. Go back and read that again if you need to.

In Genesis Chapter 12, God speaks to Abram and tells him, (God Speaking) "I will show you a land...I will make of you a great nation...I will BLESS YOU...I will make your name great...I will BLESS them that help you...I will CURSE him that hinders you....

So, we see Abram does not have to do anything...except believe GOD.

Without recapping all the scriptures again...let's just jump ahead to Galatians chapter 3. Verse 11 tells us, "The just shall live by Faith." And in verse 13-14, "Christ has redeemed us from the curse of the law, being made a curse for us...so that the Blessing of Abraham might come (on us) through Jesus Christ (so that) we might receive the promise of the Spirit through Faith."

And then in verse 16, "Now to Abraham and his seed were these promises made. He did not say, of seeds, as of many; but as of one, And to your seed, which is Christ." Then, in verse 26, "For you are ALL the Children of God by Faith in Jesus Christ.

And if you are Christ's, then you are Abraham's seed and heirs according to the promise!" In Chapter 4 verse 5 we see that Jesus came to redeem us that were under the law (cursed), so that "we might receive the adoption of sons."

THERE YOU GO...You are in the Family of God!!!

Chapter Seven

The Sower Sows the Word

In Mark chapter 4, Jesus teaches the people how the Kingdom of God operates. He teaches us a very, very important concept on how to ensure our harvest comes through.

³Hearken; Behold, there went out a sower to sow:

⁴And it came to pass, as he sowed, some fell by the way side, and the fowls of the air came and devoured it up.

⁵And some fell on stony ground, where it had not much earth; and immediately it sprang up, because it had no depth of earth:

⁶But when the sun was up, it was scorched; and because it had no root, it withered away.

⁷And some fell among thorns, and the thorns grew up, and choked it, and it yielded no fruit.

⁸And other fell on good ground, and did yield fruit that sprang up and increased; and brought forth, some thirty, and some sixty, and some an hundred.

⁹And he said unto them, He that hath ears to hear, let him hear.

¹⁰ And when he was alone, they that were about him with the twelve asked of him the parable.

¹¹ And he said unto them, Unto you it is given to know the mystery of the kingdom of God: but unto them that are without, all these things are done in parables:

¹² That seeing they may see, and not perceive; and hearing they may hear, and not understand; lest at any time they should be converted, and their sins should be forgiven them.

¹³ And he said unto them, Know ye not this parable? and how then will ye know all parables?

¹⁴ The sower soweth the word.

¹⁵ And these are they by the way side, where the word is sown; but when they have heard, Satan cometh immediately, and taketh away the word that was sown in their hearts.

¹⁶ And these are they likewise which are sown on stony ground; who, when they have heard the word, immediately receive it with gladness;

¹⁷ And have no root in themselves, and so endure but for a time: afterward, when affliction or persecution ariseth for the word's sake, immediately they are offended.

[18]And these are they which are sown among thorns; such as hear the word,

[19]And the cares of this world, and the deceitfulness of riches, and the lusts of other things entering in, choke the word, and it becometh unfruitful.

[20]And these are they which are sown on good ground; such as hear the word, and receive it, and bring forth fruit, some thirtyfold, some sixty, and some an hundred.

[21]And he said unto them, Is a candle brought to be put under a bushel, or under a bed? and not to be set on a candlestick?

[22]For there is nothing hid, which shall not be manifested; neither was any thing kept secret, but that it should come abroad.

[23]If any man have ears to hear, let him hear.

[24]And he said unto them, Take heed what ye hear: with what measure ye mete, it shall be measured to you: and unto you that hear shall more be given.

[25]For he that hath, to him shall be given: and he that hath not, from him shall be taken even that which he hath.

[26]And he said, So is the kingdom of God, as if a man should cast seed into the ground;

²⁷And should sleep, and rise night and day, and the seed should spring and grow up, he knoweth not how.

²⁸For the earth bringeth forth fruit of herself; first the blade, then the ear, after that the full corn in the ear.

²⁹But when the fruit is brought forth, immediately he putteth in the sickle, because the harvest is come.

³⁰And he said, Whereunto shall we liken the kingdom of God? or with what comparison shall we compare it?

³¹It is like a grain of mustard seed, which, when it is sown in the earth, is less than all the seeds that be in the earth:

³²But when it is sown, it groweth up, and becometh greater than all herbs, and shooteth out great branches; so that the fowls of the air may lodge under the shadow of it.

³³And with many such parables spake he the word unto them, as they were able to hear it.

³⁴But without a parable spake he not unto them: and when they were alone, he expounded all things to his disciples.

Jesus is teaching the crowds and he launches into what is **"*the most important teaching ever given to mankind.*" (emphasis mine).**

After he teaches the crowd about the "sower sows the Word," and he is alone with his twelve disciples and other followers, he is asked "What does that mean?" Jesus responds in verses 11-13 with the explanation:

¹¹And he said unto them, Unto you it is given to know the mystery of the kingdom of God: but unto them that are without, all these things are done in parables: ¹²That seeing they may see, and not perceive; and hearing they may hear, and not understand; lest at any time they should be converted, and their sins should be forgiven them.¹³And he said unto them, Know ye not this parable? and **how then will ye know all parables?**

Jesus is telling them (and us) that to understand this parable will give us understanding into how God operates, how the Kingdom of God operates and that through the understanding of this principle, people will come to enlightenment and can actually get saved! Not only that, but, just as when he came across someone using their Faith to get healed, they (and we) can "be made whole." That means a state of total restoration with nothing missing, nothing broken!

Jesus tells us, "Don't you understand this parable? How then will be able to understand all parables?" Or, rephrased, "If you can understand this parable, you will be able to understand all parables."

And remember, in verse 11, he says, "It has been given to you to know the mystery of the Kingdom of God." In other words, "It has been given to you the ability to understand how God's Kingdom operates!"

So, if we study this concept and understand it, we will be given the ability to understand "how" the Kingdom of God operates. To "know" how something operates is different from having an "understanding" of how it operates. For example, if you own a car...and you "know" that when you stick the key in the ignition and turn it, the car starts. No problem. We "know" that is how we get the car to run. But, there comes a day when you put the key in and turn it...nothing happens! Now what?

Do we say, "Well, I guess this car is broken. I have to buy a new one?" No, if you have an understanding of how the car operates, you begin to diagnose the problem. You understand that turning the key completes an electrical circuit. It allows the electrical charge in the battery to flow through the wires and activate the starter. The starter then turns the engine over.

The compression of gasoline in the engine's chamber is ignited by sparks and the engine begins to run…you release the key, disengaging the flow of electricity from the battery to the starter (because the starter is no longer needed at this point) and the car continues to run and down the road you go.

Well, if the starter is not activated when you turn the key in the ignition, there is a problem with one of three things. Either the ignition has gone out (not likely), the wiring system has gone bad (not likely) or the battery is dead (highly likely). You either get a "jump" from another battery or put a new battery in place and you are off and running! But, if you do not have an "understanding" of how that system operates, you are not able to "comprehend" this fix. You pay "good money" to someone who does understand how it operates (your mechanic).

The Kingdom of God operates the same way. If you "know" (head knowledge) how God operates, when something goes wrong, you don't know why. You have just been operating by book knowledge (this is what it says, step 1, step 2, step 3, etc. Why doesn't this work?). But if you have understanding (heart knowledge) you know not only "how" the Kingdom of God operates, but "why" it operates that way! That is when you have the ability to go to God with a need, sow your seed, and expect to get that need met.

Let's study this out a little bit...

Jesus taught in Mark chapter 4 that a sower has gone forth to sow his seed. He sowed on 4 different types of ground, but only 1 has brought in an abundant harvest. The point is, not every seed sown will give you an abundant return, unless that seed is sown into "good" ground.

Someone who sows seed "willy-nilly" is not going to receive an abundant harvest. You have to ask God for understanding and to show you which ground to sow into. And, I want to take just one more minute to explain, that not all people who plant seeds are sowers! Here is another example:

If you have a little plot of ground outside of your house, say a flower-bed. You decide this year, you are going to plant some cucumbers, peppers and tomatoes in that little flower bed. As the summer begins, the harvest is preparing itself...you see the cucumbers forming, the tomatoes forming and hanging on the vine, the peppers are beginning to grow...

Do you think any of your neighbors are going to come over to your house and exclaim, "We did not know you were a farmer!" Someone who is just planting a few seeds here and there and tending to the plants in his or her spare time is not "a farmer."

A farmer is someone who is "constantly" taking care of the field. After harvest, he is tilling into to the ground the stalks from the recent harvesting. This allows them to decay and provide nutrients to the ground. During the spring, he is constantly tilling the ground to break up the clumps of earth into fine, loose soil so the plants will have to room to grow their roots. Once he plants, he is watching over the field, nurturing it along, providing just the right amount of water at just the right time. Keeping bugs and animals out of the field as much a possible. Then, at just the right moment – he begins to harvest! He is consumed with taking care of the field in order to maximize this harvest!

Someone who just has one or two little tomato plants, a few pepper plants and a little patch of cucumbers is NOT a farmer! Because he is not "committed" to an abundant harvest and is not putting in the time nor the effort to accomplish an abundant harvest.

It is the same way with sowers in the Kingdom of God. Someone who just gives on Sunday and does not think, meditate or take action during the week to nurture, water and take care of the seed that was sown is not a SOWER, all he is doing is "scattering seed."

You see that in the first three types of ground. The first is hard ground. We could relate this to the cracks in the sidewalk. A seed may take root in there, but the heat of the day, lack of moisture and nutrients will not allow it to grow very well. It just withers and dies. Birds come and eat it up. The second type of ground is sown among rocks. The seed may find some ground beneath the rocks, but no nutrients are getting to it and it dies. The third is sown into ground that has an abundance of weeds, which take nutrients and water away from the seed and does not allow the seed to produce its maximum harvest.

But, the fourth type of ground is "good ground." It has been prepared to receive the seed. It is capable of providing the nutrients which it needs to produce a 100 FOLD Harvest! That means ABUNDANCE!

So, someone who only plops an offering down once a week is not a SOWER. He is a bucket plunker – someone who scatters his seed. Oh, he may receive a harvest every now and then, but he is not a SOWER in the true sense of the Word! To be a sower means you have to prepare yourself – before the offering is given!

Jesus has given us THE KEY to understanding how THE KINGDOM OF GOD operates! And that key is in SOWING and REAPING. In Mark 4:11, He tells us that "unto you it has been given to know the mystery of the Kingdom of God and how it operates." We have been given the right, the privilege and the ABILITY to "know" how the Kingdom of God operates. And the key to it all is the basis of Jesus' teaching that day on SOWING.

Prepare yourself and the ground.

First, you must identify what harvest you want to receive. If you want carrots, you don't plant watermelon! If you want potatoes, you don't plant corn! If you want wheat, you don't plant onions! Identify what it is you are believing for! What is it you want to receive as your harvest?

Now, you don't have to believe for finances just because you sow money. Just like you don't have to sow money to receive money. If you have worked yourself into such a huge debt that you don't have two nickels to rub together, sow your time! Or sow some clothes! God counts what you are believing for as the harvest and whatever it is you sow is named as the seed! How great is that!?

You can sow and expect a harvest as the return of a child or loved one who has left and you have not heard from in awhile. It could be the salvation of a loved one. It could be for healing. It could be for finances. It could be for a new car or new home…whatever it is you are believing for - NAME IT!

Then, **do some research.** I know this may not sound familiar to some of you who have gotten away from the Word…but this research is accomplished **by READING THE BIBLE!** Dig through the Word and identify and write down scriptures that pertain to the harvest you are believing for! If you need healing, research and write down healing scriptures. If you need finances, research and write down scriptures on financial prosperity. If you are believing for loved ones to be saved, find the salvation scriptures! This is "preparing your ground!"

Just like the farmer (sower) has identified his intended harvest and now has prepared the ground, you have identified your harvest and you are now preparing your ground! Halleluiah!

Next, you have to plant your seed. A farmer does not just go out to the field and drop his seed on the ground. The seed has to planted "just right."

It has to be the correct depth. It has to be planted in the correct manner. For example, growing up in my grandfathers home, he had a small 1 acre plot of ground which he tended to. This little plot of ground produced vegetables for the entire neighborhood! But, what I want to impress upon you is what he taught me about planting corn. In the hole he would prepare for the corn, he placed four seeds. Not one, not two, but four! This is what it would take to grow a healthy corn stalk! That same number was impressed upon me for each and every hole he had prepared for the entire row of corn. About six inches deep with four corn seeds in it, then cover it over.

So, in planting your seed into God's Kingdom, you also have to know the correct method of "planting" your seed. You do not want to just cast it out in the field and believe it gets planted! You have to "sow" the seed, not "scatter" the seed!

I recommend you take the scriptures you have previously identified and pray them over your seed. Do this BEFORE you go to church (if that is where you are sowing your seed offerings). You do not have time to pray adequately if you are trying to write down your information on the check or on the front of the envelope, the usher is waving the bucket in front of you, and the people behind your are getting impatient because the game starts in 15 minutes!

Write your check out at home and pray your scriptures over it while at home – even do it the night before. What you are doing is speaking Words of Life into that seed. It is coming alive on the inside! It is ALIVE! Get excited about sowing your seed! Don't just go to church and say, "Yes, amen, Praise the Lord, Halleluiah! Our seed is sown and now I expect my harvest to come in." But in your mind you are thinking, "I sure could have used that to pay the electric bill. My God, I still have to figure out how I'm going to buy groceries. I sure hope this sowing and reaping thing works...."

Don't do that!!! BEFORE you sow ANY seed or give ANY offering, pray and read and read and pray ALL OF THE SCRIPTURES you have researched until they become ALIVE inside of you! It is better to write your check every week (if that is how you sow your offerings at church) and just keep the check at home and then two, three or four weeks later (or months later if that is how long it takes) – when the scriptures come ALIVE inside of you and you look forward with anticipation to sowing – then GIVE the checks. *(NOTE: don't use this as an excuse to continue to use God's money to "make" it to the end of the month and then "sow" just so you could buy groceries. God knows the intent of your heart....!).*

Then, go before the Lord in prayer and present your petition before Him. I love the scripture in 1 John 5:14-15, which states, "We know that if we ask anything according to His will, He hears us; and if we know He hears us, then we know we receive the petitions we desire of Him."

A petition is "a written request...demanding a particular action from an authority or government; an appeal or request to a higher authority or being." The Bible says if we "know" Jesus hears us, then we "know" we receive the petitions we desire of Him." (Remember the teaching a little bit ago about the difference between "head" knowledge and "heart" knowledge? This is why it is important to study your scriptures you have written down pertaining to your harvest until they become "alive" inside of you, then, you KNOW you got it!).

We can make a written, formal petition and present it before Jesus through prayer. (I even take communion over my petitions). That makes it part of your Covenant! (I can hear some of you saying right now, "Oh, Brother Bob, now I am beginning to see how all of this ties together....!") As part of your covenant with Jesus, and knowing He hears you and knowing He will answer your petition, it is now time to SOW!

Now, you can give the seed you intended. Plant it! Plant it NOW! While the ground is ready! Plant it NOW, with the high expectation you have in your heart! Plant it now!!! NOW!!! Do it by FAITH! NOW! Expect the results you asked Jesus for! SOW IT NOW!

Then you have to nurture and water your seed and ground. Keeping it in maximum readiness to start to take root, grow and prosper into an abundant harvest! You do this by praying over your seed that you have sown. The Word of God is alive, it will continue to nurture your seed!

Luke 6:38 states:

Give, and it shall be given unto you; good measure, pressed down, and shaken together, and running over, shall men give into your bosom. For with the same measure that ye mete withal it shall be measured to you again.

Mark 4:20 states:

And these are they which are sown on good ground; such as hear the word, and receive it, and bring forth fruit, some thirty fold, some sixty, and some an hundred.

As your seed begins to produce, don't pluck it up before it is time to harvest! Don't dig in the ground and dig up the seed to see if it is growing! IT IS GROWING!

Mark 4:26-28 states:

26And he said, So is the kingdom of God, as if a man should cast seed into the ground 27And should sleep, and rise night and day, and the seed should spring and grow up, he knoweth not how. 28For the earth bringeth forth fruit of herself; first the blade, then the ear, after that the full corn in the ear.

So, don't dig up your seed! You gave it to God, let God grow it for you!

Next, if you have not done so already, find somebody that lives and operates by Faith and get them to pray in agreement with you about your harvest. I highly recommend doing this FIRST, before you sow your seed.

Husband and wife; wife and daughter; your best friend. Whoever will stand with you in Faith, get with them and pray in agreement over your seed, your ground and your harvest!
If you do not have anyone that you believe operates in the level of Faith you need – call or write our ministry and we will pray in agreement with you. Deuteronomy 32:20 states that one will put a thousand to flight and two will put ten thousand to flight! See what the power of agreement will do?

Finally, keep praying your scriptures, but don't keep asking God to provide your answer. It is time now to believe you already have it!

But, Brother Bob, I don't have it yet. How can I say I do? Isn't that a lie?

If you are believing for healing, can you thank God for the answer while you are still sick? If you are believing to be debt free, can you thank God for prospering you while the bill collectors are still calling? If your loved one is still lost, can you thank God for getting them saved? The short answer is – YES! Because you are made in the righteousness of God and you can operate in the same authority God has given to Jesus.

Romans 4:17 states that "God calls those things that are not as though they were." If God says "It sure is a pretty Tuesday," but your calendar says it is Friday – is God wrong?

NOPE – it is now Tuesday! God is incapable of lying, so if He says it is Tuesday – it is now Tuesday (and all of those calendars are now wrong and have to be thrown out!).

Hebrews 11:1 states:

Now faith is the substance of things hoped for, the evidence of things not seen.

Couple that with Romans 4:17 and you can see how important our words are to receiving our intended harvest.

That is why God is very careful in what He says – because what He says "comes to pass." So, go back and read Mark chapter 4 and Luke chapter 6 and Hebrews 11:1 and start to confess these scriptures over your seed!

So, when we are confessing our bills as paid; when we are confessing our loved ones are saved; when we are confessing we have our healing – we are not lying – we are speaking Words of Faith! Now, to deny the symptoms of sickness or to deny we have bills to pay is lying. If you are sick with the flu, you cannot tell someone you are not sick.

They can see you are sick. What you are denying is the flu's right to stay on your body! You can declare to the person who asks you "do you have the flu?" the following: "This sickness has no right to be on my body! Jesus bore my sickness and carried my diseases and by His stripes – I AM HEALED!" But, don't go back to bed and act like you are sick! Get up and act normal. Act like you are healed. Before long, that sickness HAS to leave your body. Because YOU ARE HEALED!

The same thing with finances are concerned. Do not deny you have bills. But you can declare, "Debt, poverty and lack are cursed under the law. But, Praise be to God, I have been REDEEMED from the curse of the law by the blood of Jesus Christ my Lord so that the Blessings of Abraham may come upon me through Jesus Christ. I have been redeemed from debt and I declare right now that by the Blessing of God – I am debt free! I receive my harvest right now to wipe debt out of my life FOREVER. I am above only and not beneath. I am the head and not the tail. I am debt free, through the Power of Jesus Christ my Lord and my Savior, whose I am and whom I serve – Halleluiah!"

The symptoms of sickness or debt may still be there. But in the Spirit, you are healed and debt free. That is why Romans 4:17 and Hebrews 11:1 are so important. We have the right to speak Words of Faith, which is the substance of the things that are hoped for and the evidence of the things we cannot see. We know we got our answers because we know He hears us and provides us with the answer to the petitions we desired of Him. We know this because we have been redeemed from the curse of the law and are under Grace. We know this because we have the Blessing of Abraham on our life. We know this because we have a covenant with God, through Jesus' sacrifice on the cross. We know this because Jesus fulfilled the promises God made to Abraham in their covenant. (Do you see how all of this is tying together?)

Well, now that the groundwork has been laid, we are ready to get to the main point of this book. That is the Seven Keys to Answered Prayer. As you go through the next chapter, keep in mind all of the foundational scriptures which we have discussed.

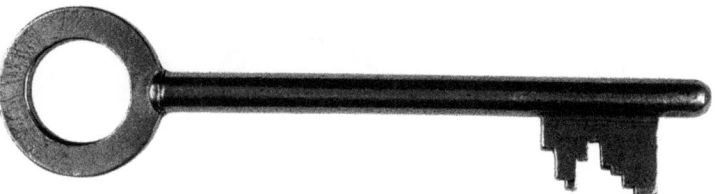

110

Chapter Eight

Don't Mess with the Mafia!

Mark 11:1-21

For this chapter, I will be paraphrasing and using my imagination for you in order to set the scene. Jesus always taught using parables so his listeners could grasp what he was teaching. I will use this method here for it is a unique way for you to get a better understanding of the situation.

In versus 1- 10, we see the story unfold of how Jesus sent two of his disciples into town to get the donkey and the colt and bring them to him. When the disciples entered the town, they found the animals tied up, just like Jesus said. When they went to untie them, the owners responded just like Jesus said they would. "Hey, what are you doing? Why are you untying the animals?"

When the disciples responded with the words Jesus told them to say (speaking the Word!), the owners responded by saying, "Oh, Ok, go ahead."

The disciples brought the animals back to Jesus, and he proceeded to ride the colt into town. The people came out in crowds, laying their clothes and palm branches along the path and proclaiming "Hosanna, Blessed is he that comes in the Name of the Lord! Hosanna in the Highest!"

This upset some of the Pharisees and the religious folks watching it unfold. They told Jesus, "stop these people from saying these things!" Jesus responded, "If they stop, these stones will start to cry it out!"

Jesus entered into town and rode right up to the Temple. He got off, gathered his disciples and they went into the outer courts. The outer courts were set up to be the worship place of the Gentiles (non-Israelites) so they could come and worship God. It was designed that way by God Himself.

But now, in this time, it was being used as a type of Bazaar for the Temple higher ups to sell items used in worship. They would sell offering sacrifices and other things to the people as they came to present themselves to the priests for the required services.

It was a Mafia style operation if there ever was one! Nobody was allowed to bring in their "own" animal for a sacrifice – even if it was perfect in every way. God commanded that the people "set aside the best" for Him. It was to be used as a sacrifice to wash away their sins. The BEST was to be killed in their place. But, when the people brought their BEST to God, the priests would not accept it. They would look it over and find any type of blemish and declare this an unacceptable sacrifice.

The people would then be referred to "cousin Vinny" where the "clean" animals were kept. "You can buy a clean animal from him." Some people traveled great distances to the required Festivals to offer their sacrifice. Now, they were either going to return home, still living in sin (in the sight of God) or they could spend some money and take care of their sin. After all, surely these animals "had to be clean." They were being sold "inside" the Temple walls!

No mention is made of what happened to the animals that were "disapproved." I suspect they were traded in...much like we would trade in a used car for a new one today. They were then taken around back, given a bath, maybe a trim, etc.

Then, tomorrow, parked out front again to sell to the next family that came to town.

Well, Jesus walks around, looking at this entire area and observing what is taking place. He doesn't say anything. It is evening; they have come a good distance today, so he tells his disciples it is time to go. So they walk to Bethany to spend the night.

Verse 12 – 19. This where the story starts to get good!

^{12}And on the morrow, when they were come from Bethany, he was hungry:

^{13}And seeing a fig tree afar off having leaves, he came, if haply he might find any thing thereon: and when he came to it, he found nothing but leaves; for the time of figs was not yet.

^{14}And Jesus answered and said unto it, No man eat fruit of thee hereafter forever. And his disciples heard it.

^{15}And they come to Jerusalem: and Jesus went into the temple, and began to cast out them that sold and bought in the temple, and overthrew the tables of the moneychangers, and the seats of them that sold doves;

¹⁶And would not suffer that any man should carry any vessel through the temple.

¹⁷And he taught, saying unto them, Is it not written, My house shall be called of all nations the house of prayer? but ye have made it a den of thieves.

¹⁸And the scribes and chief priests heard it, and sought how they might destroy him: for they feared him, because all the people was astonished at his doctrine.

¹⁹And when even was come, he went out of the city.

So, the next day, Jesus and the twelve get up in the morning and start to walk back to Jerusalem and the Temple. On the way, Jesus is getting hungry. It's breakfast time and they have not eaten yet. Jesus observed a fig tree a little way off the road and walks over to it, expecting to find possibly some "early" figs on it. He knows what time of year it is, "for the time of figs was not yet."

Now, notice something here. The tree is speaking to Jesus. Verse 14 says Jesus "answered" the tree! That tree was saying, basically, "I don't care if you are the Son of God. You are not getting anything to eat off of me! Just go on your way and starve, Jesus! You and your buddies!"

And Jesus ANSWERED the tree saying, "No man eat fruit of you hereafter forever." Then he turned and walked away. He cursed the tree right there in front of his disciples. At that moment, it died.

Now, it showed no outward signs of dying. If it would have, the disciples would have noticed it. Nope, nothing. They just turned and followed Jesus into Jerusalem.

And, when they arrived, Jesus went straight to the Temple, made a whip and started to chase the merchants out there, turning over their tables, scattering their money all over the ground! He chased away anyone who was carrying anything towards the Temple. "Is it not written, 'My house shall be called of all nations THE HOUSE OF PRAYER? But you have made it into a den of thieves!'" The Scribes and Chief Priests heard and seen these things take place. From that moment on, they sought how they could destroy (kill) him. The Bible says it is because they feared him!

Some commentators (and I agree with them) state that this incident is the one that sealed Jesus' fate. He messed with the Mafia running the Temple.

While he was "out and about" teaching the people, it was not affecting their operation. But now....He just cost them at least one day's profit. You don't mess with the Mafia's money and get away with it!

Verse 19. *And when even was come, he went out of the city.*

They walked back to Bethany. They took the same rode back as they had traveled in the morning going to the Temple. As they passed by the location of the fig tree, don't you think the disciples would have glanced over at it – just to see what had happened to the tree? There was no noticeable difference in it at that point of time. No changes at all. If there would have been a noticeable change, Peter would have spoken up (he was always speaking up about something). But nothing…just silence on the part of the disciples.

[20] *And in the morning, as they passed by, they saw the fig tree dried up from the roots.* [21] *And Peter calling to remembrance saith unto*

him, Master, behold, the fig tree which thou cursedst is withered away.

They get up in the morning and start walking back to Jerusalem. As they get to the location of the fig tree, Peter looks over and…

"Hey Jesus! Look! The fig tree you cursed yesterday – it's all withered! Look guys! Have you ever seen anything like that?" And I bet they all started to "wonder" what had happened. *(Just a side note here…the Bible says that "signs and wonders" will be done. Some by believers and some by the antichrist. The references are too numerous to go into here. I recommend you go to a good on line Bible reference and type in the key words "signs and wonders" for your own personal study on the subject. The point I want to make is, signs are for believers. For non-believers, the same miracle or sign makes them "wonder.").*

The tree had died "from the roots up." In other words, there were still leaves on it, but instead of dying "naturally" (i.e., usually the top and outer leaves wither first. This is because the tree is drawing water back to its core in order to try and survive.), this tree was withering from the roots, up the trunk and the inner leaves were dying and falling off first!

Jesus had their attention! As we get ready to study the next chapter, I want to give you the encouraging word which T.D. Jakes uses...Get Ready, Get Ready, Get Ready...!

Chapter Nine
The 7 Keys to Answered Prayers

Now, before I get into the meat of this section, I want you to understand a very important principle. You cannot limit God and there is no "Magic Formula" or incantation or anything like that which "gets" God to do something for you. God is far better than that! That is something the devil will try to get you to believe...that "you may not be saying the right thing," or "you're saying it wrong."

The purpose of this section is to show you how to "activate" your Faith. It is designed to show you and lead you into a format of "believing you receive as you pray." If you "say" you believe you receive, and then turn right around and tell your spouse, "well, I hope that worked...," you might as well give up and go home...because it didn't work and NEVER will work. For a double minded man will not receive "anything" from the Lord (James 1:7). You either believe it, or you don't believe it. There is no "maybe" with God.

To summarize what we studied earlier...Jesus taught the crowd about the Sower Sows the Word. He then explained in detail to his disciples how the Kingdom of God operates according to this principle of Seed Time and Harvest.

He taught them at great length about how to tap into the Faith of God, activate their Faith, and believe...He has been teaching them how Faith works, how the Kingdom of God provides for every need...they have seen miracles; they have seen him healing everyone who has come to him; they have seen him walk through crowds (and taking them with him) when they wanted to stone him or push him off of cliffs....

And Jesus used it as a teachable moment. In doing so, He also gives us the "7 Keys to Answered Prayers!"

First, you must have Faith In God (Mark 11:22). In order to have Faith in God, you first must believe that God IS GOD! Hebrews 11:6 tells us that "But without Faith it is impossible to please him (God): for he that comes to God must believe that He is (God), and that He (God) is a rewarder of them that DELIGENTLY seek Him." That means you have to believe that God is in control! You have to believe that God's Word is true! You have to believe that God cannot lie and that if you find a promise from God to you written in the Word, it belongs to you!

Johns 17:17 says "Thy Word is Truth." Jesus said in John 8:32 "you will know the truth (the Word) and the truth (the Word) will make you free." To be made free means you are released from bondage. So, if you are in financial bondage, physical bondage, sickness, disease, relationship – whatever type of bondage you are in, the Truth (the Word) will make you free! One translation says it this way, "the Truth you KNOW will make you free!" Because, if the Word says, for example, "by His stripes you are healed," but you don't know the Bible says that, you cannot walk in that truth because you don't know it. But, once you KNOW that is what the Bible says, you CAN walk in it – and receive your healing!

Also, in 1John 5:14-15, we see that if we "ask anything according to His will (and God's Word is His will), then we know He (God) hears us; and if we know He hears us, then we KNOW we receive the petitions we desire of Him."

So, we must have FAITH IN GOD…that is Key number ONE!

Second, we must believe we receive the answer to the prayer request we made to God. Jesus says in Mark 11:23 "whosoever shall SAY to this mountain (whatever mountain is looming in your life that you are trying to move and asking

God to remove for you), be thou removed and be thou cast into the sea; and shall not doubt in his heart, but shall BELIEVE that those things which he says shall come to pass; he shall have whatsoever he says…"

Again, we must BELIEVE that we receive AS WE PRAY. You cannot say, "if it is your will…" because if we base our prayer on what we find in God's Word, we have already discovered IT IS HIS WILL! If we find it, and His Word is true, it belongs to us. First Corinthians 1:20 says "For all the promises of God in Him (Jesus) are YES and in Him (Jesus) AMEN." So all the promises we find in God's Word are for us. And when we find them and stand on them without wavering, God's Word for us is "YES – AMEN!" (Now, in case you did not know it – AMEN does not mean "that's the end of my prayer." It means "SO BE IT." It is a most powerful Faith statement that "religion" has made just a "cute little saying we add at the end of a prayer so everyone knows we are finished." NO, AMEN means SO BE IT! It is a powerful Faith Statement that makes it a FINAL, UNCOMPROMISING STATEMENT!

So, Jesus says if we base our prayer on what we find in God's Word, and believe that what we find in God's Word is a promise made from God to us, and we base our prayer on these promises, we can believe that God will answer them. The mountains that are looming over us will begin to move…we have God's promise that it is so!

Third, we must be in agreement. We have already studied about getting into agreement with the Word of God, with His promises. But, we should also get into agreement with each other. It is so vitally important, especially for a husband and wife, to come together in agreement. We have several scriptures that talk about the power of agreement, but two right off are Matthew 18:19 and also John 14:14. ("Again, I say unto you, that if two of you shall agree on earth as touching anything that they shall ask, if shall be done for them of my Father in Heaven…If you shall ask anything in my Name, I will do it.").

Fourth, we must TAKE the answer to our prayer. Kenneth Copeland gave a very vivid picture of what this means. If someone presents you a tray of cookies, and asks you "would you like a cookie?" and you respond with, "Yes," then you reach out and TAKE the cookie.

Receiving answered prayer is the same way. You find the answer to your problem in the Word of God, you have FAITH in the Word, you believe you receive the answer, you are praying in agreement and you TAKE the answer by Faith...

Fifth, Mark 11:24 says to believe you "receive and you shall have..." If you receive something, you take possession of it. And once you have possession of something, **you HAVE IT**.

But Brother Bob, I don't actually have the answer yet. I am still sick or still in debt – whatever the case may be...You must TAKE the answer by FAITH...Hebrews 11:1 states, "Now, Faith is the substance of the things that are hoped for and the evidence of the things not seen." By using your Faith, you are activating the substance of the thing you are praying for and holding onto it as the evidence (proof) that you have something you cannot yet see!

When God created the universe and everything in it, He did it by Faith...He spoke what He wanted to come to pass and it was just as He said. He said, "Light BE...and light was!" (Genesis 1:3). God's Words were the "substance" of something (light) which was not yet seen. But light was made by God "speaking" it into being, by Faith.

We have the mind of Christ. We have been made into the Righteousness of God because of what Jesus did on the cross. His death, burial and resurrection satisfied the requirement for punishment on mankind in the eyes of God. He "became sin" for us so we could become Righteous in the eyes of God. Therefore, "The Word is near you, even in your mouth, and in your heart: that is, the Word of Faith, which we preach." So, TAKE the answer by Faith and start talking about it as though it was already manifested!

When you do that, you HAVE the answer (you just can't see it yet...but it is there – by Faith). Faith is "creating" the "thing you have hoped for." And, if you HAVE it, that means you already possess it! Think back to our "cookie" example. Once you "take" the cookie, who has possession of it? It is no longer on the tray, it is in your hand. YOU HAVE IT.

But, Brother Bob, if it is being created by Faith, then I still don't "have" it, do I? YES, you do! You have taken the answer by Faith and you HAVE the answer by Faith. God will move Heaven and earth to get what you need into your hands when you stand in Faith.

Remember the Prophet Elijah? When he killed all of the false prophets, Jezebel told him he would be dead by the morning! God told him to RUN! And then God told him to go by the stream and he would provide for him. What did God do, he had the ravens bring Elijah food twice a day!

God could order the birds to gather up all of the lost coins in parking lots and drop them overnight into your front yard! Do you think that would pay off your debts? Jesus told Peter to go fishing when they needed tax money. Do you think He could tell you to go fishing and give you $10,000?

I know, for a fact, a situation where this happened, when I was at Jerry Savelle Ministries International Bible College in Crowley, Texas. An instructor by the name of Dick Rueben was a guest speaker. He is an awesome instructor, especially on the subject of the Ark of God. He is a Jewish Christian and was not "brought up" in the Word of Faith. He was asking Brother Jerry Savelle some things about faith and finances and sowing and reaping.

Brother Jerry was showing him about the story where Jesus told Peter to go fishing and take the money out of the mouth of the first fish he caught (Matthew 17:24).

Brother Rueben asked, "Do you think God would actually use a fish like that?" Jerry told him that if God would do it for one person, He would do it for any person because God is not a respecter of persons."

Anyway, a few days later, Dick Rueben was visiting some relatives in Alabama and was asked if he wanted to go fishing. He agreed and the two went out on the lake. A little while later, Dick got a bite and when he hauled in the fish, it had a tag on it. The friend said this was the "tagged fish" that was put into the lake as part of a contest and everyone had been trying to catch that fish for several weeks! When they turned it in, Dick got the $10,000 prize! You cannot talk Dick Rueben out of his Faith in how God works!

If you want to drive the devil nuts, start talking and walking by Faith. You ask God for an increase in your finances and the devil will tell you that you did not get it. You just quote the Word to that rascal and stand in Faith. You tell him, "I got...I got it and you can't see it, HA! HA! I got it devil, I got it and you can't even see it!" Refuse to give up. Are you going to believe God or are you going to believe the devil?

When he tells you that you don't have it, tell him he is a liar and the father of lies. So if he says you DON'T have it, that means you DO have it! God's Word is the TRUTH. God's Word says you have the answer – and God's Word is the Truth. The devil says you don't have it, and he is a liar! There you go!!!! YOU HAVE THE ANSWER!!!!

(When you start to laugh at the devil, telling him you have the answer to the prayer and the devil can't see it; when the devil tells you that the answer has not come and you tell him he is a liar – so if he says you don't have it that means you do you have it – you get him so twisted up he can't think straight. Then, he leaves!)

Sticking with our "cookie" analogy, after you take the cookie, and you now have the cookie, what is the usual thing a polite person will say – "thank you."

So, the Sixth Key is to thank God for the answer! Start to Praise Him for coming through for you. The scripture says "God inhabits the Praise of Israel (His people)." (Psalms 22:3). We are His people...so Praise HIM! Be BOLD enough to Praise God and see if He shows up! HE WILL!!!

And then, in Mark 11:25-26, we see probably the MOST important key to receiving from God. **The Seventh Key is this. "And when you stand praying, FORGIVE,** if you have aught (or anything) against any (person), so that your Father also which is in Heaven may forgive you your trespasses. But, if you do not forgive, neither will your Father which is in Heaven, forgive your trespasses."

Unforgiveness will STOP the Blessing of God from reaching you. You MUST make a quality decision to FORGIVE. "But Brother Bob, you don't know what those people did to me…" You're right – I don't. And I don't want to know and I don't need to know…and you need to stop rehearsing in your own mind and ears what they did to you.

Let me ask you this…What is the absolute WORST thing you have ever done in your life? Something that NOBODY knows about and if they found out about it would embarrass you (and maybe put you in prison because of it)? Whatever it is, guess what? God already knows about it. But, I have good news for you. Jesus paid the price for that transgression. You are Forgiven!

If you have accepted Jesus as your Lord and Savior and asked Him to forgive you of all sin in your life – that sin, no matter what it was, was forgiven! When you confess your sins to God is not when He finds out about them, it is when you get rid of them!

Jesus taught His disciples to pray in Luke 11:4, "Forgive us our sins as we forgive our debtors." Or, in the NIV, "forgive us our sins as we forgive those who sin against us." If we have been forgiven greatly, we should also forgive greatly. There is no holding back on forgiveness. You must make the decision to forgive, no matter what. The devil will try to say, "Yeah, but…" You must tell the devil, "No, I have already made the decision to forgive that person. As far as I am concerned, it never happened. You go talk to God about it. I refuse to dwell on it anymore."

The following quote is taken from Paul Sibley's website and perfectly sums up what we are talking about: *After we've asked the Father to provide for our needs, we go on to ask for pardon: "Forgive us our sins." "Forgive" follows "give." The two petitions are linked by Jesus, "give us today our daily bread" with "forgive us our sins as we forgive those who sin against us."*

By linking them we recognize our need for pardon when we think of our need for food. Also, as we confess our own guilt, we bring to mind our relationships with other people too.

Augustine called this request, "the terrible petition." If we pray, "Forgive us our sins as we forgive those who sin against us" while at the same time harboring an unforgiving spirit, we are actually asking God not to forgive us. You are part of the forgiven fellowship if you honestly know God as your Father. Sometimes it's hard to forgive some particularly damaging thing done to you. But the sins we do against God, which we ask forgiveness for, make others' offences against us much more trivial. How can we ask God to forgive us, when we refuse to forgive others? Our forgiveness of others doesn't cause God to forgive us. Rather, it is evidence that we, ourselves, have entered into God's forgiveness. Those who live in the relief of God's pardon find it easier to forgive those who offend them.

It's said that, "to sin is human, to forgive divine." We're never closer to God's grace than when we admit our sin and cry out for pardon. And we're never more like God than when, for Jesus Christ's sake, we extend forgiveness freely and completely to those who have sinned against us.
(Paul Sibley, www.paulsibley.net/2008/11/06)

"When we extend forgiveness freely and completely to those who have sinned against us" is when are the most like God. That is absolutely the most important thing for you to take from this study. FORGIVE those who have done you wrong. That puts you into a position where GOD CAN BLESS YOU!

Chapter Ten

Conclusion

In summary, The 7 Keys to Answered Prayer are:

1. Have Faith in God.
2. Believe that you Receive as you Pray.
3. Put yourself in agreement with God's Word and, if possible, with another believer.
4. Take your answer by Faith.
5. Have (or possess) your answer (by Faith if necessary, but do not give in to pressure to say you "don't" have the answer).
6. Begin to Thank Jesus for answering your prayer request and Praise Him.
7. Make the quality decision to forgive!

If you have ever wondered what it took to "get" God to answer your prayers, you now have the Seven Keys to Answered Prayer. These seven keys are not a formula or a "system" to "get" God to do something. These keys are the foundation upon which you can build a scriptural foundation that you can rely on. A foundation upon which the devil has no ability, nor authority to destroy. A Spiritual foundation upon which you can drive your stake in the ground and tell the devil "NO MORE!"

I pray that you have learned how to activate your Faith in God's Word by the study we just completed. It is my heartfelt prayer that the scriptural basis upon which this book was written will help you in establishing your prayer foundation and that it motivates you to do your own scripture study to build upon.

God's Word will go forth and not return to Him void, "but it shall accomplish that which I please and it shall prosper whereto I send it." (Isaiah 55:11).

If you base your prayers strictly upon the Word of God and the promises made by God in His Word to you, then your prayer requests are scriptural. If your prayers are scriptural, then they are in the Will of God.

Example Prayer of Petition for Finances

"If you ask anything according to His will, He hears us; and if we know He hears us, then we know we have the petitions that we desire of Him." (1John 5:14-15).

If you form your prayer along the basis of this example, it will be scriptural. I urge you to go through the Bible for yourself. Dig into the Word. Find scriptures in the area you are praying for. This example is based up financial needs, but you can use it for healing, relationships, etc. All you have to do is substitute the appropriate scriptures for the financial scriptures:

Father in Heaven, I come before your Throne of Grace and Mercy today, to obtain Mercy and to find your Grace to help in our time of need. Father, in the Name of Jesus, I ask for your Blessing on this prayer request today. Jesus, you promised in your Word in John 14:14 that whatever I ask in your Name, the Father would do for us.

My spouse and I present this petition before you today, requesting the amount of $_____. In honor of this harvest, I plant the seed of $_____. I am believing for a one hundred fold return based upon Mark 4:20. We are tithers, according to Malachi 3:10. We are sowers according to Mark chapter 4 and we are givers according to Luke 6:38.

We tithe out of obedience to your Word. And Malachi 3:10 says you will "open the windows of Heaven and pour us out Blessings that we do not have room enough to receive them all." In Malachi 3:11, you promise us that you will "rebuke the devourer for our sake." So devil, you have been rebuked! Father, your Word says in Matthew 18:18 that whatever we "bind on earth will be bound in Heaven." So devil, in the Name of Jesus, I bind you from touching my finances or my harvest of $_____. God has rebuked you because I am a tither and I bind you in the Name of Jesus because I am a saved child of the Living God!

Father, we sow into your Kingdom by planting financial seed into other ministries. Mark 4:14 tells us the "sower sows the Word." So, as we sow financial seed, we are assisting these other ministries as they are preaching the Gospel. And, we are believing for a hundred-fold return on every seed which is sown.

And, Father, we are givers. We give out of Love, for God is Love. We give according to Luke 6:38 and we believe that when we "give, it shall be given to us again, good measure, pressed down, shaken together and running over shall other men give into our bosom."

Father, I know this prayer request is based upon your Word and your Word is true. For John 17:17 tells me "Thy Word is Truth." And, since it based upon your Word, then I know it is according to your will. And, since it is according to your will, then I know you hear me and if you hear me, then I know I receive the answer to this petition that I desire of you.

Now Father, again, in Matthew 18:18, it is written that whatever I "loose on earth is loosed in Heaven." So I loose my angels that have been sent to minister to my every need to gather up my harvest of $_____ and put it into my hands. This is because Hebrews 1:14 states these ministering, spirit angels are sent "forth to minister to the heirs of salvation," and that means me.

Father, I know that debt, poverty and lack are cursed under the law. But, I have been redeemed from the curse of the law and I am under Grace, because Galatians 3:13-14 states that "Christ has redeemed me from the curse of the law, being made a curse for me for it is written, 'cursed is everyone that hangs on a tree' so that the Blessing of Abraham might come upon ME through Jesus Christ that I might receive the promise of the Spirit through Faith."

Therefore, Father, I declare the Blessing is active in my life, according to Deuteronomy 28: 1-14. I am Blessed coming in and going out. I am Blessed in the city and in the field. My family is Blessed, our home is Blessed, my job is Blessed and our finances are Blessed. I am the head and not the tail and I am above only and not beneath. All that my hand touches is Blessed by the Lord my God, in the Name of Jesus.

That is why I can stand, by Faith, on Mark chapter 11, verses 22-26 because:
I have Faith in God and in God's Word. Jesus, you are the Word of God made flesh, so I have Faith in You. I believe with all of my heart that the petitions I request are coming to pass – NOW – in my life. Hebrews 11:1 says, "Now – Faith IS..."

And it is the "Substance" of these things I have asked you for and this Faith IS the proof of these things, even though I cannot see them right now. I have them NOW. I have my harvest of $_____ NOW. My wife and I are in agreement with each other and with the Word of God. Therefore, we TAKE the answers by Faith. And since we take the answers, that means we have the answers NOW, because NOW FAITH IS…therefore, Father, I thank you and I Praise you for the answers to our prayers. And Lord, I forgive. I make a quality decision to forgive. If I have anything in my heart against anyone, Lord, I make the decision to forgive, as I have been forgiven.

Thank you Father for hearing my prayers and thank you for the answers to my prayers. In Jesus Name, AMEN (SO BE IT).

Signed this date _____

_____   _____

Evangelist, Pastor and Teacher –
Robert Thibodeau

Freedom Through Faith Ministries (FTFM) has been proclaiming and teaching the Word of God since 1999 when Robert R. Thibodeau (Brother Bob) founded the ministry in Fort Worth, Texas. He is the founder and current director of the ministry, which has been located in Baltimore, Maryland since 2001. Since the inception of FTFM, Brother Bob has worked with other ministries in the conduct of crusades and large-scale concerts all across America. He has seen healings and miracles take place during these events, and has realized what the Power of God can do in a persons life once they accept Jesus as Lord! With Faith in God, all things are possible to him who believes!

The primary purpose of FTFM is to evangelize, disciple, teach and empower people everywhere to impact their world with the Gospel of Jesus Christ. "Brother Bob" does this by introducing them to Jesus as their Savior and motivating them to apply Biblical Principles in their everyday life.

In addition to his weekly radio broadcasts on selected radio stations located in various parts of the United States, Brother Bob has a weekly Internet radio broadcast, which is heard around the world. The Internet broadcast is primarily focused on ministering to the former Eastern Bloc and surrounding countries, China, the Middle East and African nations. Although the broadcast is currently only in English, translations of the website is made in 8 different languages!

As always, we pray for our Partners on a daily basis. YOU are the most important aspect of this Ministry. YOU are the reason we share the Gospel of Jesus Christ and what He did for us on the Cross. YOU are the reason JESUS IS LORD!

Remember, "Be of Good cheer, for Jesus has overcome the world (and all the problems of the world). And this is the Victory that overcomes the world" - your Faith and our Faith in agreement together!

For more information on Robert Thibodeau and Freedom Through Faith Ministries, please visit our website at **www.FTFM.org**.

www.ingramcontent.com/pod-product-compliance
Lightning Source LLC
Chambersburg PA
CBHW071659040426
42446CB00011B/1840